GRAUEL

GRAUEL

Reverend John Stanley Grauel
An Autobiography
As Told To
Eleanor Elfenbein

IVORY HOUSE

FREEHOLD, NEW JERSEY

Printed and Manufactured in the United States of America by Haddon Craftsmen, Inc.
First Printing January 1983
Designed by Barbara Van Vliet,
Riverside Design Associates, Inc.
Jacket photograph by Ed Kelly
Library of Congress Catalog Number: 82-090188
ISBN 0-9608896-0-4

My deep appreciation for my good fortune to have Dr. Edward T. Byrnes of Seton Hall University as my editor and to Toni Mendez for encouragement and advice when much needed.

To my mother and all of those who were supportive and
believed as I believe
J. S. Grauel

TABLE OF CONTENTS

LIST OF ILLUSTRATIONS

FOREWORD

The pages that follow bear the flat, single dimensional, printed letters spelling out the facts, figures, conditions and incidents of a man's life. Only as the reader responds will that life reach its true proportion. This is the story of an individual whose place in the history of Israel can never be disputed. He never reached high office or honor, or held positions guaranteeing constant world press coverage and yet his devotion and dedication to the cause have set an indelible stamp on the creation and continuing history of Israel. I am aware that his contribution and concern for humanity go far beyond the needs of my country, but it is his place in the history of Israel with which I am most familiar.

John Grauel came on the scene over thirty years ago. I met him on a number of occasions in the United States as David Ben Gurion assigned me and others to set up the framework of organizations to assist the eventual creation of Israel. He worked with us in many ways but his contribution was greatest as he articulated our needs by speaking all over America. Then at one point he disappeared. Months later the Yishuv was electrified by the report that the largest refugee ship of the "illegal" blockade running period, loaded with thousands of people, was steaming into Haifa Harbor, after having fought a bitter battle with the British fleet.

Her name was "Exodus." Her history has been recounted over and over again. Bartley Crum, a member of the Anglo-American Commission concerning the Palestine question, called her, "the ship that launched a nation." From that cruelly battered wreckage, as she finally made the harbor, emerged John Grauel. He had spent seven months on that ship. His contribution during that period has been set down by witnesses. The greater contribution came as we engineered his escape from the British police and brought him before the United Nations Commission then meeting in Palestine.

Golda Meir, in a speech to the Jewish Agency, referred to his testimony as the first appeal by a "priest, a perfectly worthy gentile, a priori, no Jewish witness was to be believed," and because of this, his graphic account became a turning point in the attitudes of the U.N. representatives. In the records of the sessions these prophetic words emerge. "Finally, I would like to make this statement, gentlemen. I have watched these people. I know what they are and I tell you, the Jews in the European Displaced Persons Camps insist on coming to Palestine. They will come to Palestine and nothing short of open warfare and complete destruction will halt them."

Incidentally, in Hebrew there is no distinction between Catholic and Protestant clergymen. In Golda Meir's speech she referred to John Grauel as the "komer," the priest. Thus, he is known in Israel as Jochanan Ha Komer, John the Priest, and the title is uniquely his.

He has not ceased his efforts. In later years most of his efforts have been dedicated to working with young people. Thousands of youthful visitors have heard him speak through the United Jewish Appeal sponsored program, "Operation Joshua." Hundreds of visitors have listened to his lectures in the stark Yad Vashem, the Jerusalem memorial for the millions murdered by Hitler.

Rev. John Grauel is a familiar figure in Jerusalem, the city he

FOREWORD

regards as his second home. He always wears white and around his neck is the ever present Cross of Jerusalem. He is usually followed by a stream of youngsters as he recounts the wonders of "his city."

In 1974 I was privileged to present him with the Medal of Jerusalem, an honor which carries deep meaning. I know what he really wants. His life and dedication have been a prayer "for the peace of Jerusalem."

Teddy Kollek
Jerusalem, July 1977

PROLOGUE

I stood behind the railing on the bridge of the Exodus —1947, as tugs nudged her battered hulk into the port of Haifa. The quay was swarming with British sailors, soldiers and marines. Leaning over I could see for the first time, the extensive damage done to us by the British destroyers during the battle ended only a few hours ago.

Suddenly, from a sea door where a ramp had been placed, a stretcher was being carried out and I recognized the body of Yacubovich, the fifteen year old who had been murdered by the British. The blankets were rolled down to the waist and the head bandaged to appear as though he were still alive. I cried out in anger and frustration, "That's the most goddamned, despicable trick I have ever seen pulled." I shouted so loud that I drew the attention of a number of British officers below. One of them called out, "Come down. Now."

I gathered together a few items I wanted to salvage and made my way through the ship. As I moved along, some of the poor, exhausted refugees made way for me, many of them reaching out to touch me. The slimy decks were covered with people sprawled out, overcome by the overpowering combination of the fetid July

heat and the stench of the stopped up toilets. As I passed, someone called out, "Give 'em Hell!"

I came down the gangway to be met by the officers and taken
to a car. As we drove slowly through a mass of people pressing
against the fenders, I saw soldiers standing guard, some carrying
fixed bayonets. The car turned right and in a few minutes I was
in front of a building surrounded by barbed wire and sand bags.
A sign read "Palestine Police, Haifa." I was escorted into the
building, down a hallway, and brought before a lieutenant seated
behind a desk. He looked at me for a few seconds then, "Papers."
I reached into my pockets and handed him my passport contain-
ing a visa I had secured in Paris three months ago, permitting me
to enter Palestine. I also turned over to him a few inconsequential
items but held on to five thousand dollars in cash.

"Do you have any money?"

I put the money on the desk. He looked at it, saying, "Why
are you carrying so much money?"

Not finding myself in a cell and my confidence somewhat
restored, I resorted to flippancy. "I'm an American. I don't like
travelers checks and I'd rather pay for everything in cash."

He opened my passport and looked up at me in surprise. "You
have permission from the Palestine police to enter Palestine."

"Of course. I'm a newspaperman."

There was a letter folded in the back of the passport which he
opened and read. It was from John McCormack, Majority Leader
of the U.S. House of Representatives, an old friend of mine, and
had no bearing on my present situation, but it was written on
official stationery, made reference to Matt Connelly, secretary to
President Truman, and written in a personal vein addressing me
by my middle name, Stanley. The only reason I kept the letter
was a poem on the back copied from the *Paris Herald*.

The lieutenant read the letter, thought a bit, and then put in
a phone call the gist of which was, "We have a United States

newspaperman here with a visa to enter Palestine endorsed by the Palestine police. He is carrying a large sum of money and has a letter on official stationery referring to the White House."

I could not catch any of the staccato reply coming from whatever source of omnipotence he was consulting at the moment. He slammed the phone down in its cradle and said crisply, "His Majesty's government is placing you under arrest."

My first reaction was one of shock, but I recovered enough to say, "I want to contact the American Ambassador."

"Do you imagine that the American Ambassador is going to come all the way down here from Jerusalem just to consult with you?"

"If he doesn't, he'll be spending the next year in the consulate in Iceland," I snapped back, hoping to brazen through the situation.

He picked up the phone again, repeated that I was demanding the presence of the American Ambassador, asked for further instructions, listened, turned to me and announced, "I will have to detain you in a cell."

"If you put me in a cell, you will have to answer to my government. You will also have to use force to lock me up."

Another phone call, a few more exchanges, and His Majesty's government decided to keep my papers and place me under house arrest in the local hotel. With a police escort we started to walk the few blocks to the Hotel Savoy.

"Good God," I thought. "I'm under arrest in the land of Palestine, the Holy Land, Terra Sancta." I thought of the seven tense, exhausting months of the *Exodus* affair, its tragic ending, and the hope filled years of preparation that led up to this moment. "What am I doing here? I should be coming to this land as a Christian on a pilgrimage."

I had dedicated my life to the Methodist ministry and here I was walking with a British military escort, under arrest in a far off place about which I knew little beyond its' biblical history. This was not my fight. What was I doing involving myself with these Jews? The officers at my side were my mother's people. One of them may well be Welsh like my grandparents. My own culture was founded in Britain, not in this ancient, alien land. The closest I had ever come to being arrested was when I would go speeding around my parish and would be admonished by our police to slow down because I was needed.

CHAPTER 1

DEPRESSION AND LOSS

Sooner or later in my relationship with people the question arises, "How did a white anglo-saxon Methodist minister get so deeply involved with the Jewish people and Israel?" My shortest, most frequently given answer is, "My mother inflicted me with a social conscience." Actually, that is true, but hardly the whole story. Nothing as complex as my life could be so simply motivated.

I was born on December 12, 1917 and for reasons never given me, my mother walked a long way to the hospital on a cold and blustery night with the snow crunching under her wet shoes and cold feet. She told me years later she thought that walk to the Hanneman Hospital in Worcester, Massachusetts would be her last journey. I never knew my mother's parents except through family reminiscences. Her father was a shoemaker from England who settled in Prince Edward Island in Canada. He had nine children of whom two died of diphtheria, leaving my mother with five sisters and a brother. My father was second generation German, his mother having come from Saxemeiniger, Bavaria. She was married in New York to a man six years her junior whom she had met on board ship when they were both coming to the U.S.A. I was told that my paternal grandfather was a very fastidious

1

gentleman and my grandmother was an indifferent housekeeper. They had two sons one year apart and after the second son was born my grandfather disappeared into oblivion.

My mother was small, blonde, and determined, a person of boundless energy and enthusiasm. Deeply religious, she was a teetotaler who thought that playing cards on the table meant the devil's cloven foot was under the table. On one occasion she did not talk to my father for three days because he had drunk a glass of beer. Years later she loved the eggnogs I would make at family gatherings, and I never had the heart to tell her I did not use rum flavoring as she assumed. Three drinks and she would nap happily on the couch much to the amusement of her five sisters, none of whom shared her taboo on alcohol.

She was a strong advocate of the brotherhood of man and lived her convictions. Back in the thirties when a black man and white woman raised a storm in the church by announcing their intentions to marry, my mother offered our home for the wedding. She also had a very mystical feeling about the Jewish community. As I was growing up, she frequently observed that anyone on the side of the Jews would survive any of life's vicissitudes because the Jews were God's Chosen People. She was convinced Judaism must survive because it was the root of her own faith. It is my own deep conviction that the death of Israel would be the death knell of Western Civilization.

My mother would not tolerate gossip at the dinner table. We had to exchange ideas and sometimes the subjects were rather graphic for a young child. I never forgot one meal during which mother took the opportunity to share the news about the Russians being murdered in the Ukraine at the time of a famine, and the horror of dead bodies being shoved into a culvert. Mother knew how to impart information with all its worth and dramatic impact.

My father was a strong six footer and a hard worker with a quick temper. He had a swarthy complexion, a Roman nose, and a head

DEPRESSION AND LOSS

of black, curly hair. I inherited my six feet one from my father and my light coloring from my mother. I would like to think my temperament came from my mother too, but I suspect a touch of father's hairtrigger temper has shown itself now and again. Once, on a job, a fellow worker told my father he looked like a Turk. I do not know why my father regarded that as offensive, but he took after the poor guy with a wrench. As I recall the story, no damage was done on either side. I also remember a visit from one of father's closest friends, a railroad brakeman he grew up with in a ghetto on Liberty Street in Worcester. He and my father used to go cat fishing on Saturday nights. I remember catching at his hand one night and saying, "Charley, my friends told me you're a nigger." My father immediately gave me a very simple and unforgettable lecture on man's multifaceted racial origins and beliefs and the fairness of judging people as individuals.

Up until 1929 it was a grand time to be growing up. My brother George, 13 months younger, and I were surrounded by a loving and close family. We were constantly on the go, all our activities centering around the church. Radios provided entertainment and were not a problem to obtain. If you could not afford to buy a two tube Crosley, you could make your own crystal set. I remember my father weeping with joy and excitement because he could hear President Calvin Coolidge speaking from New York City.

We would visit Concord and Lexington and many other places that supplied free entrance to museums. I was already an independent brat and would often take off alone to spend the day at the Peabody Museum, in Salem, Massachusetts, where I would sop up huge doses of history. My family never worried. I would reappear in the evening and tell them where I had been. To this day I am an early American History enthusiast.

Then in 1929 the depression hit us personally and my father became unemployable. He was a skilled steel die stamper for custom stationery, and elaborate stationery became a casualty of

3

the economic bust. We lost our house and my parents told George and me we were poor. It came as a shock. I remember the summers we spent living in a tent on a farm in Shrewsbury, Massachusetts. At night Mother would read to us from Dickens. She loved reading and had an enormous capacity to learn poetry and could recite it by the yard. After the daylight was gone and the candle burned out she would continue to describe book plots and recite poetry. I loved it. What were trying times for my parents were a delight for me.

After that came a succession of jobs from one town to the other where I went from one school to another. We did a variety of things to keep going. From door to door we sold pot holders and pin cushions which Mother had made. We harvested tobacco in South Windsor, Connecticut, picked cranberries in Cape Cod, and strawberries somewhere else. We were migrant workers although I did not identify that occupation by name until years later. Finally Mother decided to run an inn in Pittsfield, Massachusetts, since in addition to a job it would supply us with a home. It was a glorious period for all of us while it lasted because there was always a tremendous amount of food for the taking in the refrigerator. That philosophy, the depression, and my parents' inexperience made it one of the briefest hotel careers in history lasting about one hectic year. So it went, from place to place with the names of the towns blurred by the passage of time. All I clearly recall was that I thought only the unfortunate lived in stationary homes without the adventures and travels we poor people enjoyed.

Looking back now, the years between 1929 and 1932 were tough and lean, but we never starved physically or spiritually. We took great pride in the fact that we never needed public assistance. There was a rule in the household that if our parents, either out working or looking for work, were not home by four o'clock, George and I had to put up the potatoes, our dietary staple.

DEPRESSION AND LOSS

Somehow my mother always found something to go with them. Like the story they tell about the poor on Prince Edward Island who could always live on potatoes and point. While they ate the potatoes, they would point at the codfish hanging from the ceiling and manage to get by.

Winter brought Franklin Delano Roosevelt as president and the subsequent bank holiday found father and me swapping mother's sewing output for food to sustain us. We managed to get through that winter, but in the spring father decided he had to go someplace else to find work. Feeling his luck might change in the south, we headed for Florida. We got as far as Washington, D.C. where thousands of unemployed squatters had built a camp on the ground now occupied by the Pentagon. I spent my time during those spring days, fifteen years old and carefree, wandering around the city, loving our capital and sightseeing every corner of it.

One day while passing the White House I got an inspiration. In those days the White House was simply guarded by a lone sentry box and guard at the gate on Lafayette Avenue, instead of the trappings of today's security sensitive bureaucracy. I nodded to the guard as I passed him, continued to the door, and entered the office building to the right of the White House. No one seemed at all concerned or tried to stop me. I walked over to the nearest desk and told a man who asked what I wanted that I was there to ask President Roosevelt for a job for my father. He asked me to wait. I remember sitting down near a gift of the Philippine government, a table with legs made to look like the heads of water buffalo.

A tall man came over to me, introduced himself as Mr. Sturling and asked if he could help me. I told him at length about my family's problems and he asked me to wait. He came back shortly with a man he introduced as Mr. Steven Early who looked me over then took down all my information on a little white pad, and again I was asked to wait. Mr. Early returned in a short while and requested that I come back to see him the next morning. Still without saying anything to my parents, I came back as directed. Mr. Early gave me a letter for my father to present in person to an assistant secretary of the Department of the Interior. I went back to the camp and told my father what I had done and gave him the unsealed letter to read. We immediately went to see the man the letter was addressed to, who questioned my father and asked him to return the next morning at 10:00 A.M. Father kept that appointment alone. How excited we were when he came home and told us we were moving to Virginia where he was to be employed by the Department of the Interior in the creation of a new state park. My father turned to me saying, "Sometimes I don't understand you. The man who gave me the appointment told me that the reason I got the job was because White House head of Secret Service, Sturling, and Steven Early, secretary to the President, were so impressed with my son's faith that his request would be fulfilled that they couldn't disappoint him." Everyone was a little appalled at my audacity in going directly to the President for help. All my life I have continued going right to the top to get things done when I thought there was no other recourse. Rarely have I been disappointed in the response. As soon as my father received his appointment we were on our way to Cape Henry, Virginia.

Once settled in Virginia, with the help of a Methodist minister, Benjamin Bland of Virginia Beach, I entered Randolph-Macon Military Academy, a Methodist school at Front Royal, Virginia. I spent two happy years there completing my high school education as a pre-ministerial student of the church. I graduated from the academy in June, 1936, and we moved to Colonial Beach, Virginia where my mother took over a small store that sold various sundries and necessities to the black community immediately behind us. She was trying to raise the money necessary to put me through college. In the fall I enrolled as a pre-theological student in Randolph Macon College, Ashland, Virginia, a continuation of the educational system of the Methodist church.

During this period my father had been working as a supervisor in the state park he had been assigned to. It was a CCC project, one of President Roosevelt's efforts to solve the high unemployment problem of the depression. The Civilian Conservation Corps was made up of the unemployed and often unemployable young people, many from the inner cities, who were put to work on conservation projects around the country building parks and play areas. My father taught those city boys how to swing an ax and survive in the woods, skills they never learned on city streets. While on the job, my father suffered a severe fall on his elbow and a month later, in the spring, he was found to have melanomic carcinoma. I left school in May to help my mother keep things going and made many a sad journey from Colonial Beach to Baltimore, Maryland where he was being treated in the Marine Hospital.

In July, in an effort to save his life, they performed what is known as a shoulder and girdle operation, which meant the removal of his left arm and his left breast. He came home in the fall, and we went fishing together. I did my best to keep him cheerful, but the cancer spread and after being treated in the hospital for a time, my mother decided the best place for him would be at home in Massachusetts where he would be surrounded by his relatives and friends. He was admitted to the Chelsea Marine Hospital near Boston where he died on Thanksgiving Day. He was buried in the Hope Cemetery in Worcester to the accompaniment of the Wellington Rifles Firing Squad of his National Guard unit. He was 49 years old.

Quite a number of people showed up at the wake. I did not know many of them, but my mother introduced me to Judge

Charles Murphy who had been a friend of my father's. I was to learn later that the judge was a member in good standing of the state political machine. He asked me what I planned to do in the future.

"I really don't know," I said. "I've been studying for the ministry."

"What do you do best?"

"Well, I think I have a gift of gab."

He snorted, "Well, you can do one of two things with that gift. You can either sell insurance, or go into politics. Come to my office tomorrow."

The following day I called on Judge Murphy and he told me about James Michael Curley, who had been governor of Massachusetts and was running again and would I come down the following day and have lunch with the Governor? So, there I was, 19 years old, not at all prepared to meet prominent people, having lunch in the Hotel Bancroft in Worcester with the former governor of my state. Governor Curley studied me across the table for a bit, then suddenly asked, "Would you like to work with me? Would you like to introduce me this evening?"

I said I would be delighted and that evening in Mechanics Hall I introduced the man who had been, and hoped to be again, the governor of Massachusetts. I do not remember quite what I said that night, but I do know that a cheer went up from the audience, and for the first time I experienced the thrill of applause. When the evening was over, the Governor approached me and said, "Son, come to see me at my home tomorrow night." He pushed a twenty dollar bill into my hand.

The next evening I found my way to Boston with the help of the twenty dollar bill and went to 350 Jamaica Way, a red brick house with shamrocks on the blinds. A uniformed maid answered my ring, showed me into a hallway where she took my very thin coat, and left me in a study with book lined walls, every single

8

book bound in the same binding. As I looked around the title, *The Autobiography of Benito Mussolini* caught my eye. I took it down, opened it, and there on the flyleaf was inscribed, "To my friend His Excellency the Governor of Massachusetts, James Michael Curley", signed Benito Mussolini, Il Duce. I started to read the book, and I do not know how long I spent thumbing through the pages, reading snatches here and there, when I felt a presence. I looked up to see the Governor dressed in hickory trousers, tails and a bowtie.

"What are you reading?"

The Autobiography of Mussolini.

"What do you think of him?"

I replied, "Governor, he's certainly stuck on himself."

He thought for a moment, then, "Young man, unless you really believe in yourself, whatever your calling in life, you will never succeed."

Thus, my first taste of politics and politicians. Heady fare for a youngster fresh out of Chipwamsic Swamp, Virginia.

CHAPTER 2

EDUCATION AND PACIFISM

With my father gone, and me anxious to make my own way, Mother packed up and took herself and my brother off to Florida with bus money she managed to scrape up. There she found work as a Practical Nurse. I did not quite know what I was going to do because obviously at 19, floating around the edges of Massachusetts politics was hardly enough to sustain me. Then I met Donald Smith, secretary of the Worcester YMCA. He was one of the most remarkable individuals I have ever met, and if anyone other than my parents ever had any kind of influence upon me, it was Smitty. He had me taking care of groups of kids within the context of the Y programs, and I realized in later years that many of the jobs he gave me he created for me.

Smitty had two camps, one on Nantucket Island, the other in Hyannisport, both adjacent to golf courses. He ran the camps during the summer to give poor youngsters jobs as caddies, charging them the bare minimum for room and board and making enough money to keep the camps functioning. I became associated with the camp as a sort of right hand to Smitty and during the summer I became the cook at the Hyannisport Camp. Years later, after I became involved with the Jewish community and traveling far afield, I would use my vacation time to go back

10

to cook at the camp and give Smitty a hand.

It was through Smitty that I became acquainted with the Kennedy family. Smitty cashed in his life insurance, having no dependents, and bought a fifty year old Friendship sloop from Sterling Hayden, who was later to become famous as an actor and author. I helped Smitty fix up the sloop, and we went sailing as often as possible. Smitty, at the request of Joe Kennedy, had taught the Kennedy boys how to swim. I thought of that when the reports came out of the war about John Kennedy swimming three miles from his PT boat to get help for his comrades. John Kennedy and I were the same age. He was a very attractive looking and personable young man even then. I never got to know Bobby Kennedy too well. He was just a young boy on the dock who seemed to spend all of his time fighting with his brothers, with the townies, with the caddy camp boys, and anyone else who came within reach of his fists. Teddy at that time was just a fat little baby always underfoot.

The Kennedys had their own theatre at home, and on Saturday nights the camp boys were all invited over for a movie. The refreshments that followed were always the same. A large peanut butter sandwich. It was part of Hyannisport gossip in those days that the Kennedys were sometimes years in arrears with their local grocery bills, and the outstanding feature of those bills were amazingly large quantities of peanut butter. They lived very haphazardly those summers. They were all athletes, swimming, boating, sailing, and playing the inevitable touch football. Meals would often mean a dash into the house for gobs of peanut butter on thick slabs of bread and out of the house on the run again. I believe that marriage to Jacqueline Kennedy smoothed some of the rough edges off the President. I do not think his own inclination would have run to the French cooking served in the White House during his occupancy.

Once in a while Joe Kennedy used to turn up on the golf course.

Legend had it that he did not like to pay a caddy and that is why he would wander off by himself with two clubs, a driver and a putter, and always play alone. One fall while I was still at the camp, my mother came to visit me. Not understanding about golf courses and having picked up a love of napping out of doors from our tenting days, she chose to nap on a well mowed fairway. She came in to tell me that she awoke, "to find a very strange man out there staring down at me." I glanced out the window to see Joe Kennedy walking away in the distance. I explained to my mother that, "first, you weren't supposed to sleep on the fairway and second, that strange man was Joseph Kennedy, our Ambassador to the Court of St. James." She was very unimpressed.

The Kennedys supported St. Francis By The Sea Catholic Church, and one summer the church held an auction and garage sale. I had begun to acquire an interest in antiques and went with some friends having been told there would be some interesting glass available. There was a Victorian monstrosity everyone seemed to be interested in and bidding was vigorous. I leaned over and asked an old lady what all the excitement was about and she said, "That's the Kennedy cradle. All the children have slept in it." I shrugged my shoulders. I showed the same perspicacity later at the seminary, when Dr. Charles Cummings, a very great teacher and professor of Hebrew at Bangor Seminary, offered me a choice of Hebrew or Greek. I chose Greek thinking I was interested in archaeology, but what would I ever do with Hebrew? Today I do not remember much more than the Greek alphabet, but I sure could have used the Hebrew.

I was very busy handling a heavy schedule alternating between the Caddy Camp, the YMCA, and politics. I was functioning as one of Governor Curley's campaign representatives, which in less impressive jargon meant I covered political functions that were not important enough for him to attend in person. Whenever I had the opportunity I would spend time listening, fascinated, to the man who would one day be the focal point for *The Last Hurrah* and titled his own autobiography, *I Would Do It Again.* The Governor not only taught me a great deal about making speeches, but I remember the days when he would gather his staff around him for a drink and entertain us with stories he told with barbed wit.

One of the people he disliked most was Cardinal William O'Connel of Boston whom he referred to as "gangplank Willie." The Governor insisted the only time the Cardinal appeared in public outside his cathedral was when he was standing on the gangplank going to or coming from one of his too numerous Bermuda vacations. He never forgave the Cardinal for allegedly fighting against child labor laws, and attributed the Cardinal's views to extensive factory investments.

Curley was a brilliant, self-educated man who hated the entrenched hierarchy that ran the state, the Saltonstalls, Cabots, and Lodges. I remember one speech in which he said the fattest graveyards this side of China were around Lowell and Lawrence, Massachusetts. He claimed they were filled with the uncounted, wasted bodies of women and children who had worked in the mills owned by these distinguished state leaders. He delighted in pointing out that they boasted of their patriotic ancestors, the founding fathers of the Saltonstalls, Cabots, and Lodges, but failed to mention that many of them ducked the American Revolution by sitting it out in Nova Scotia, while leaving their business affairs in the hands of managers. Curley also liked to remind his listeners that many of the wealthy leaders of the state inherited fortunes made in the trading of rum, slaves, and sugar.

I think James Michael Curley was one of the greater personalities on the American political scene, and it always bothered me that he was considered a brigand and a pirate. That description is much too simple and one dimensional. He grew up in Boston under the political tutelage of Martin Dever, uncle of Paul Dever who would succeed Curley as Governor. Curley became entrenched in the system of ward politics, yet was fiercely honest in every sense in terms of his relationship with his fellow man. He appeared to be tall, though he was not. He was always impeccably dressed, sometimes in a velvet Prince Albert suit, big grey fedora, an ever present cigar, and an enormous chain across his ample paunch. He carried pockets full of silver dollars which he dispensed to various admirers and shoeshine boys.

Typical of the way Curley handled things was the way he would hold court to hear from his constituents. People would line up outside his office and be passed through the door a few at a time. About half a dozen members of his staff stood at the ready as Curley listened to requests, juggling a few at a time, ordering one staff member to put in a phone call for him while another was sent to find needed papers. It was an exercise in organized chaos. One could argue with great cynicism and considerable truth that he was concerned about future votes. Fair enough. Would that today's politicians were as concerned about the niggling problems of their voters. The people loved him because he made them feel that they existed as individuals.

One little old lady came to complain that she had been fired as a cleaning woman from the Worcester State Hospital, the implication being that she had been fired by a WASP supervisor. Not to lose time, Curley had an aide get the hospital supervisor on the phone while he handled the next supplicant. The hospital connection was made, Curley picked up the phone, "I want to speak to you about Mrs. O'Leary." Silence as he listened, then Curley replied, "Yes, I am the Governor of Massachusetts; and if you're the Queen of Sheba, let me tell your majesty that you will have to find a new kingdom unless Mrs. O'Leary is back on the job immediately."

James Curley lost the gubernatorial election in 1938, but I was already established in the lower echelons of the Democratic Party

EDUCATION AND PACIFISM

of Massachusetts and held a series of politically appointed jobs. In the fall of 1939 I became a deputy sheriff under Oscar Rocheleau, sheriff of Worcester County. It was the time of the South Barre strike, when there was a fierce jurisdictional labor battle between an outside union and a local union at the Barre Woolcombing Plant. I was furnished with a double barrelled shotgun and a steel helmet, which offended my sensibilities and my social conscience, but I was pragmatic enough to realize I needed the fifteen dollars a day. That was big money in those early days. For me the only good thing about that strike was meeting Jack Walsh, who enhanced my interest and concern for Ireland. He was an older man, a veteran of the Irish Rebellions of 1916 and 1922, and we became good friends. When his tongue was loosened with enough whiskey, he would entertain for hours with stories and songs of the traditions of Ireland and the Rebellions.

The strike was a battle between Yorkshire men from England and Italians who were laborers in lesser jobs at the plant. We learned that there was to be a confrontation between the Italians who wanted to join a national union and the British who wanted a local union. Nine of us were assigned to stand guard between the two groups on a slope leading up to the area where the Brits lived. We were standing around, helmeted and armed, when two large groups started to move toward us, the English in front of us and the Italians behind. Jack and I favored peaceful reconciliation, but the next few minutes found us caught up in a rock throwing spree. A girl immediately in front of me was hit between the shoulder blades with a big boulder, the resulting sound like the snap of a splintered cheese box. I made the decision that this was no place for me. Using my club and flailing in all directions, I fought my way through the group, which by now was fighting in deadly earnest with whatever weapons came to hand, and pushed my way to the top of a slope and away from the fight. The only amusing thing about the whole business was that for years

I was being reminded of my heroism in wading through the battle. All I was trying to do was get out as fast as possible, but the legend kept building in spite of my disclaimers. I am still bumping into reminders of my heroic exploits at the Battle of South Barre. The strike was settled with a great deal of publicity in the local papers, and I went back to Worcester, my brief career as a deputy sheriff at an end.

All through the winter my father's pastor, Dr. George Heath of the Wesley Methodist Church, came to talk to me from time to time about going back into the ministry. I finally yielded to the pressure from my mother and Dr. Heath. When I arrived at the seminary, I was questioned by an inquisitorial committee of professors who were very curious about my background because my reputation had preceded me in terms of my association with Curley. As a result of the interview I was accepted at Bangor Theological Seminary, Maine, a school with an unusual program dedicated to training men for the rural ministry. It was the fall of 1941 and the eve of the United States entry into World War II, and men were in short supply, so arrangements were made to study for the ministry at the seminary but with University of Maine professors. Finding me reasonably articulate they assigned me to a church the first week and at the end of three weeks I was pastor of a parish in North Brewer, Maine while I continued with my studies.

Along with everyone else who has lived through that period I will always remember the afternoon of Dec. 7, 1941. I was taking a nap and was suddenly jarred awake by loud banging on my door. One of my student friends informed me that the Japanese had bombed Pearl Harbor. My immediate response was "where is Pearl Harbor?" I did not immediately grasp the implications of the news. War! Coincidentally, just before Dec. 7th, there was a request from A.J. Muste, head of the "Fellowship For Reconciliation" to address the seminarians. I can still recall how enraged

EDUCATION AND PACIFISM

I was and still am now thinking of how Dr. Harry Trust and his neanderthal British education would not permit an acknowledged pacifist to appear at the school to speak to the student body.

Several of the professors and a number of students were members of the Fellowship and I was incensed at the efforts to stifle discussion and dissent. In my anger I declared that under the *Constitution Of The United States* my home was my castle and barring any unruly or unreasonable activity I could legally hold a meeting in my chambers which consisted of two small bedrooms and a larger study room. Dec. 8th the day of Pres. Roosevelt's *Day Of Infamy* speech in which he declared war on Japan, the Fellowship met in my rooms. It was a custom of Dr. Trust's to hold a periodic quiet hour when he would give a small homily for us to ponder. After the Fellowship meeting several of the students asked me to join them in the chapel for a quiet hour which was scheduled for the purpose of coming to terms with the impending war.

Dr. Trust took that opportunity to dress us down for accepting the 4D classification automatically given to divinity students, and in gung ho British tradition informed us that the time would come when we would regret the privileged status that prevented our being called for active duty. I was furious and with my customary disregard for the amenities when I am in a temper I interrupted the hour to challenge Dr. Trust's remarks reminding him we had come together for the purpose of gathering our thoughts and making judgments and it was hardly necessary for him to impugn our patriotism. He was annoyed, looked grim and sat down.

I must have redeemed myself in his sight when I gained a measure of prominence due to my activities on the *Exodus.* When we met several years later he hastened to remind me that he was British and after all the British were really historically responsible for the creation of Zionism. If this was true I wish the

17

attitude had continued on to that point in time when I found myself literally staring down the business ends of British guns. I am reminded of Churchill's remark that he was a Christian Zionist, a state of mind he always exhibited when out of office. Most politicians can manage to be for almost anything until they attain positions of power and authority.

I was a member of the "Fellowship of Reconciliation" from the spring of 1941 until the fall of 1942 but I was uneasy wearing the mantle of pacifism. I always had a belligerent response when seeing people pushed around and my instincts to get involved kept me in and out of trouble all my life. While I would never resort to the taking of life I could not stretch pacifism to cover the times when I have resorted to a little force to "pacify" a situation or two.

After much discussion, debate and meditation the die was cast for many of the students. There were those who remained absolutely opposed to war and I recall one professor who was eased out of his position because he was totally against war. I have always believed the taking of life is wrong. To me life is sacrosanct and yet there have been times when I know I have been indirectly responsible for loss of life by virtue of my Zionist activities. I am also mindful as Rabbi Joachim Prinz said at one point in time, the ultimate sin may be that of silence when to speak out could save lives. Several of my friends chose to go to war as conscientious objectors and in those years paid a price for their concern for the salvation of human life.

As for me I have decided I have a split personality. There are times when I can be totally at peace with myself such as a time after my father's death, when I stood before an apple tree in full bloom and wept looking at the beauty of the tree while thinking of my father who so enjoyed nature. There have often been times when I have been so profoundly at peace I am sure there was not one antagonistic cell in my body. Yet on other occasions I can respond quite physically, sometimes to the point of endangering myself and others when I see people being abused.

There have always been those in high places aware of the sins of war yet pragmatic enough to compromise to the point of insisting salvation lay in strength of arms rather than in peace. I think there is a depravity in man. Some choose to call it original sin; even popes and I use the term symbolically to include all those exalted religious leaders who have compromised their principles when they blessed the armies going off to war to kill or be killed, assuring them that God is on their side whatever cause they choose to champion. I am apocalyptic about the future yet I cannot sit back and give up as I am so often tempted to do. The hurt is there but I would hurt a great deal more if I did not keep trying to make changes; to make a difference. You must go on even if only to save your own soul. Giving up would be a concession to all the forces of evil.

It was 1943 and I was in my last year at the seminary; a year which was to be one of the most devastating periods of my life. I saw an attractive young woman named Meg in a local restaurant and being naturally friendly it was not difficult to become acquainted. She had a job and small apartment in town and I began sneaking out at night from time to time to visit her. The rumor mill at the school reached Dr. Trust with the information and I was called in to give an account of my behavior. I compounded the problem. I was twenty-six years old and resented what I regarded as an unwarranted intrusion upon my personal life. I denied the rumor knowing if I admitted to its truth I would be leaving myself open to one of Dr. Trust's long lectures on morality which he delivered without one iota of understanding or compassion. My friendship with Meg continued and to our dismay Meg became pregnant. We immediately went to a friend on the faculty who married us in a very private ceremony. We felt when the time was propitious we would announce the event.

GRAUEL

The months flew and to my great distress it became apparent that Meg was suffering from a pre-natal depression, a condition more prevalent in those days, and had to be placed under medical care in Bangor State Hospital. I consulted with several doctors especially Dr. Alexander Dodd in whom I placed great confidence. While still hospitalized Meg went into labor and in the process of a complicated delivery I lost both Meg and my son in childbirth. I went through the agony of their loss alone since no one had as yet been notified of our marriage. My own mother and family were not told until years later. My visions of what might have been and my sense of loss and guilt have been recurring threads darting in and out of my life.

I managed to pull myself together with the help of Dr. Dodd but I was haunted for many weeks by strange dreams one of which having nothing to do with my wife and child but with my father who had passed away several years before. In my dream I was wandering around in an area of swamps and tummock—little hills of grass. Upon one of those little hills quite high above the water and almost inaccessible was my father's coffin and my hope was that somewhere in the general area I would find a shovel with which to bury the casket. In the dream I realized as I was searching for a shovel that I could not succeed in digging a grave in a watery swamp. Dr. Dodd interpreted my dream as being on two levels, one being my own disappointment as to the way my life was progressing. The second part of the dream was expressing my own feeling of not fulfilling my father's hopes for my success in some particular part of my life.

The second dream took place in a dentist's chair while I was under anesthesia preparatory to having some teeth extracted. The dentist's office was near the city hall from which a loud speaker was broadcasting Christmas carols. In my dream I was traveling on a barge up a canal that was full of twists and turns. On both banks there were Christmas trees and I could hear Christmas carols. Suddenly I stopped at a small island upon which stood a young, handsome, blonde lad whom I immediately identified as my son. I awoke at that point needing no help from Dr. Dodd to interpret that dream. Over the years when I grew tired or discouraged the dream would frequently appear.

When my father died, I being the eldest son and in spite of my youth, became the head of the family. It was the custom in those days of primogeniture for the widow to step back and make way for the eldest son. In my case family meant not only mother and brother George but a large family of aunts, uncles and cousins as well as weddings, funerals, non-functioning furnaces and lawn mowers. Later on when I became a minister I was expected not only to be the fount of all wisdom but a pipeline to God. All my life I have had people looking to me for help and as a consequence have found it difficult to look to others in terms of my own needs. I still find it impossible to talk over very personal situations and difficulties with anyone, relying totally on my own resources to solve my problems, often to my own detriment.

My brother George made a career of the army and after retirement became a Salvation Army worker, married a Salvation Army lassie and they have a daughter Sheila. George, a conservative, religious man leading an orderly life, never could fathom my way of life and my devotion to Israel. It would be a gross understatement to say we have conflicting life styles. Although I had the great pleasure of officiating at my niece's wedding and the warmth of a family reunion, my travels around the country and Israel keep us apart. As a result an important part of my life has been lonely, especially around Thanksgiving, Christmas and Easter.

The peripatetic nature of my life made it difficult for me to contemplate remarriage during my younger years. Later, in addition to the fact that I still traveled a great deal, illness plagued me culminating in two operations for cancer. I had always imagined the progression of my life would lead to a traditional groaning board surrounded by a wife, children, relatives and friends. That not being the case everyone's children are my children.

CHAPTER 3

FROM PULPIT TO POLITICS

In 1942 I was assigned to a five community church in Stonington, Maine, a magnificently beautiful spot in Penobscot Bay. Stonington and the surrounding four small islands that made up my parish are granite outcroppings and extremely difficult places in which to live. My boating experience in Hyannisport came in very handy. To cover my parish and for sightseeing as well, I would borrow an outboard motor boat and go out alone, much to the consternation of my parishioners, who always regarded me as a landlubber. As I look back on it now, it was a pretty risky thing to do in those unfamiliar waters since the boat was simply a dory with a motor. I would take along extra gasoline and visit around or just plain wander over the islands climbing up the rock outcroppings to find an osprey's nest, meeting with an angry mother who came at me with the wrath of a winged fury as she protected her fledglings.

The total water supply in town was dependent on the rainy season and stored in cisterns in the cellars of the houses. Only the very wealthy had flush toilets. Until its discovery by tourists in more recent years, the major industry on their several islands was fishing. At the time I arrived, England was beginning to buy large supplies of fish to augment her scanty rations during World War

GRAUEL

II. Once in awhile, you would come upon someone lucky enough to own a touch of green earth in this rocky paradise who was trying to coax a garden to life. The island was sparsely populated by inbred, taciturn people who fiercely guarded their privacy. So long had they been cut off from the mainland, that their English still bore an Elizabethan tinge. Communication was by boat and not too frequent, especially during the long winters which ran from twenty to thirty degrees below zero. Strangers were not easily accepted. It took me six months to gain general approval in spite of the fact that I came pre-packaged with a church imprimatur.

Andrew Richards, Father Polequin, and I were the clergymen on the island. My salary from the church was $13 a week and I do not think Andrew was receiving much more from the Congregationalists. Father Polequin survived on what he could get from the last fifteen Italian families in the area. The Italian colony had been a thriving one when the famous Stonington Stonecutting Quarry was in operation. This is the granite quarry that supplied the basin for the statue of Prometheus in front of New York City's Rockefeller Plaza. The demand for quarry stone had diminished to the point where the few remaining Italian families and Father Polequin were having a very rough time.

It could have been worse. The Father and I enjoyed some status in the community, and one of our lobster fishermen saw to it that every Saturday we received over half a bushel of lobsters along with other choice items of the fruits of the sea. Stonington abounded in lobster, scallops, haddock, cod, and hake. Father Polequin and I would get together on Saturdays, eat only the tails and the claws and throw the rest away. Such luxurious waste! Lobster then was about twenty-eight cents a pound and it was a delightful experience to eat just the choicest parts. Whatever else could be said about that period of my life, there was always plenty of food.

FROM PULPIT TO POLITICS

My two years at Stonington were for the most part a couple of the liveliest and zaniest of my life. Two of my closest friends on the island were the local undertakers, the Jones Boys. The island was dry, so the Jones Boys were also the local bootleggers. Occasionally, we would have a death on one of the islands in the dead of winter, and using one of the heavier fishing boats, with the temperature at thirty below, the wind howling, and the boat soon covered with several inches of ice, we went to the funeral. Sometimes it was so cold there would be no question of embalming. We would simply go into the room of the deceased, throw open the windows and the elements would take care of the body in a few hours. After that we would load the deceased and the family on the boat, putting the casket in the hold and head for the mainland for burial. Once in awhile we would have to chip the ice off the casket and let it lie above ground for as much as five days before interment. On other occasions the casket would wait only long enough for the grave diggers to open the frozen ground, with very generous portions of the Jones Boys' corn whiskey giving added impetus to the picks and shovels.

I had picked up some knowledge of embalming. One day, coincidentally, we had three deaths at once and each Jones took one body and they left the third to me. I guess they were not concerned about my lack of experience since my client was a welfare case and there would be no complaints from his family. It was one of our terribly cold days and I decided to light a fire in the potbellied stove before I went to work. I threw in some paper, wood, and added a match. There was a loud explosion and Bob Jones came tearing into the room yelling, "Dammit, you've just blown up our supply of whiskey for the week." It had been hidden in the bottom of the stove.

That was only part of the insanity around. One of the parishioners, a dear old lady, always looked forward to my visits when she would repeat for the umpteenth time her entire funeral service planned down to the last detail, including the poems she wanted read and the clothes she would wear. Suddenly her twin sister died and got the whole show, dress, pre-selected poems and casket, while she sat in church and enjoyed the funeral. I regret not knowing whether she planned a whole new service for herself, or being pleased with the first, scheduled a re-run after I had left the parish.

The church was jammed all the time on Sunday nights, not mornings, because days I also filled in on the fishing boats and trawlers when they needed an additional man, which was frequently. It meant extra money for me. We would lay three miles of gear, seven or eight tubs with hooks every thirty inches and then haul in the fish. The captain got one third, the crew including me got a third, and the boat got a third. In addition, I also filled in at the fire department for $5 a fire, and I was broadcasting once a week on station WABI in Bangor. I did not have a car, not being able to afford one, so I commuted by thumb, hitching a ride on anything with wheels going in the right direction, including the 3 A.M. lobster trucks. It was rugged but marvelous training for me years later when I would be on land and sea with the Israeli underground rescue missions, and my endurance would be taxed on more than one occasion.

I enjoyed my life and the people of Deere Isle, and I believe we respected each other. I learned to live by their customs and traditions, but it was not always easy. They were very close-mouthed and occasionally when there was a lobster war, someone would get shot, and the whole island population would suffer from acute amnesia. When the body would appear and the state police were called, I suffered from the same condition, knowing as little as everyone else, for the sake of maintaining my relationship with the people. I felt it was my obligation to help prevent these incidents, not apprehend the culprits. On the lighter side, once in awhile I was more privy to a situation than the rest of the community. A member of my church, a 70 year old married man, was carrying on a romance with a 69 year old widowed lady of Father Polequin's church. She lived a door or two away from me, and I would hear the gravel crunch outside my window as her lover sneaked into her window at night and again when he left in the morning. Father Polequin and I would get together and the greetings were, "How's the romance?" My answer would be, "You're in a better position to know. She has to confess to you. There's nothing in my church that compels it."

All during this time I was following the news from Germany and was very distressed by pictures in the papers of Nazi thugs standing over old Jews scrubbing the streets of Berlin. While suffering this abuse and other indignities, the Jews were wearing their Iron Crosses won in defense of Germany during World War I. So much did I find this disturbing that I would talk on the air about what was happening and there were frequent complaints to the station about my "defend the Jews" kick. I clearly recall that the world was not too upset about Hitler's excesses either, and any outcry from the clergy, if any, must have been made in whispers. The politicians for the most part were confining themselves to non-partisan, placating noises. They were busy concentrating on the "Red Menace" represented by Soviet Russia. Perhaps I was more sensitive to what was happening to the Jewish community because of my friendship with Judge Joseph Goldberg of Worcester. He was of Russian-Jewish background and vice-president of a national Zionist organization. In answer to my questions he gave me books to read on Zionism and awakened my interest in the search for a Jewish homeland.

There were two Jewish families in Stonington. One ran the hardware store, the other the fruit and vegetable store. The morning of July 4, 1943 I came into town, which consisted of a few stores, the post office, and that day, what seemed to be the entire population of Stonington waiting for the steamer to bring the mail. They all saw it. Sometime before dawn the windows of the fruit store were smashed, the produce strewn all over the street, and across Levy's door and the stone step leading to it was scrawled the word "JEW." I went to the town constable, Reuben Cousins, who was the functioning police force, and expressed my feelings of outrage. I tried to explain how terrible this demonstration was in human terms. On the eve of July 4th, as on Halloween, he commented, the local kids had a habit of tearing up property. They would put a dory up on the rooftop, or fill a buggy with hay, set it afire, and send it careening down a hill. This, Cousins insisted, was just another such harmless prank.

When he refused to do anything to apprehend the kids, if indeed they were kids, I went to consult with Andrew Richards and together we went back to ask Cousins for help. When he refused, we told him if something was not done immediately we would clean up ourselves. He scoffed at the idea. Andrew and I went back, picked up Father Polequin, and the three of us dressed in our church robes and carrying buckets of water and brooms went back to clean up the street and scrub off the word Jew. Immediately people started to pitch in and help. Levy, who had stayed in the back of the store in shock and terror, came out and started to clean up, too. Cousins finally joined us by taking a swipe at a vegetable or two, but with little enthusiasm. We only had one small weekly paper in town and to the eternal credit of the publisher, Gordon Mackay, he published an editorial the following Saturday that was entitled, "We Hold These Truths To Be Self Evident Now As In 1776."

I believe there is a built-in anti-Semitism in a large part of the social structure of the WASP community. It is not only anti-Semitic, but as in the case of a small, enclosed and entrenched community like Stonington was, it is anti-anything that is on the periphery of their way of life. If it is different, it is suspect. For instance, when several of the elders of my church in Stonington got wind of my friendship with Governor Curley, they were horrified. Their kindest opinion of him was that he was some kind of Robin Hood. Worse than that, he committed the ultimate sin. He was a Catholic.

The only tensions in the community came from the Mormon sect called The Church of Jesus Christ of Latter Day Saints Re-organized who belonged to the Independence Missouri Church, not the Utah Church. They maintained a very aloof attitude toward the rest of the community. I could understand why. They insisted they were God's elect, and they had already fenced off the gravel area in Independence to mark the exact spot of the landing of the feet of Jesus in the second coming of the Messiah. I suspect I would be inclined to be stand-offish myself, with an inside track like that. It sort of reminds me of the Russelites who grew out of the Methodist Church in the 19th century. They set the exact time for the coming of Jesus, sold their property, sewed on their ascension robes, and gathered one morning on the rooftops to wait. The incident is true, but one apocryphal aspect of it might be the story told of one old man. It was said he did come garbed in his ascension robes, but he also carried an ax. When questioned about the ax he answered, "Well, Brother, if Jesus isn't here by twelve o'clock as prescribed, I'm going out to cut the winter's wood." I am not given to dates for prophetic accomplishments myself, never having had anything fall on schedule in my entire life, so far.

After Stonington, I was routinely shifted to another church, but I was increasingly restless and frustrated. Pearl Harbor had exploded, and we were at war. I was exempt from the draft because I was a clergyman, but I was still a member of the "Fellowship of Reconciliation" headed by A. J. Muste and by definition, a pacifist. I had to search my conscience, my very soul. A clear cut choice was not necessary to my peace of mind. I could acknowledge the country's need to defend itself but could not see myself in any area of combat. I went back home to be with my family and to make my decision.

The stories coming out of Europe about refugees, Jews, all the excesses of the Nazis, were haunting me. I finally decided to ask the church to relieve me of parish duties and to permit me to work in areas in which I felt I could make a more significant contribution. I called Judge Goldberg, informed him of my decision, and asked him as my Zionist mentor, what he could suggest. He sent me to see Dr. Carl Herman Voss, of the American-Christian Palestine Committee. Created in 1943, this was a national organization tied in with the Zionist Emergency Council to help create a Jewish State. Headed by Senator Robert Taft of Ohio and Senator Robert Wagner of New York, it had the support of such prominent people as John McCormack, Majority Leader of the House of Representatives, Senator Owen Brewster of Maine, Reverend Daniel Poling of Philadelphia, Monsignor Ryan of Chicago, Reverend Howard Lesourd, Dean of the Boston University Graduate School, and other very distinguished citizens. These men apparently felt Zionism was an idea whose time had come, and this was where I felt I would like to have some impact.

Dr. Voss suggested I go to Boston because they were looking for someone there to function as executive director of the Children To Palestine, a Christian group formed to assist the Youth Aliyah program of Hadassah to rescue Jewish children from the hell of Europe. I was interviewed by an aging, slightly deaf, sweet lady, on of all places, Joy Street, in Boston. Joy Street always reminds me of the two old Boston ladies discussing the poor economy, their dwindling finances, and a mutual friend who became a prostitute. "Well," decided one of the women after some thought, "that's better than dipping into the principal."

The interview was pleasant enough, but I was turned down because of my background and resultant lack of experience. I have

FROM PULPIT TO POLITICS

no idea what kind of experience was required under these unusually cosmic circumstances, but I reported back to Dr. Voss. He offered me the Executive Directorship of the Philadelphia office of the American-Christian Palestine Committee. This was not the combat I had in mind, but it would have to do until I learned more about myself in terms of what I had to give and the niche I wanted to occupy. Never in my wildest, most unrealistic projections into the future, could I have divined the direction my life would take.

The post of Executive Director operated out of an office in the North American Building, and I found myself with a desk job. I wandered around to women's teas, preached sermons in churches, and mailed out pamphlets. I was also snowed under by the enormous amount of paper work that is usually the by-product of entrenched interests. Due to my love for American history I enjoyed Philadelphia, but I cannot say the people of the City of Brotherly Love returned the affection. I met dozens, if not hundreds of people during my stay, but not once in seven months was I ever invited to have lunch or dinner with anyone. I used to entertain myself by walking up and down Chestnut and Market Streets and indulge my interest in the antiques in the store windows. Things got more interesting when the Committee and the Zionist Emergency Council decided to set up a lobby in Washington for the creation of a Jewish State. I lived there for some months working with Meyer Weisgal who one day would become the president of the Weizmann Institute in Israel, Rabbi Joshua L. Liebman, who is best known in the gentile community for his book *Peace of Mind,* and a number of other Zionist dignitaries. We were hoping to get a majority recommendation from the Senate asking for the creation of a Jewish Commonwealth.

I went to see Senator Taft to ask him to sign the proposal as a member of the American-Christian Palestine Committee, sure

31

of his cooperation. He heard my request, went into another room, returned furiously with a letter he almost threw at me, and demanded that I read it. The letter was from Rabbi Abba Hillel Silver referring to a previous meeting with the senator and reminding him that what was wanted was not a recommendation, but a resolution from the Senate committing that body to an outright request for a Jewish state. This would not be the first instance I would find of the lack of consensus in the Jewish hierarchy. Senator Taft, apparently supporting Rabbi Silver, continued to berate me, the committee, and the Zionist Emergency Council for this conflict. I went back to the headquarters of our lobby group and reported my experiences, feeling that in most instances Senator Taft was a gentle, courteous man, not given to intemperate outbutsts. I raised that point and questioned the senator's allegiance to the Rabbi rather than to the committee. I was told that Rabbi Silver was reported to have engineered a political pact with Democrat Governor Frank Lausche of Ohio that there would be no interference with his political future if he did not interfere with Republican Robert Taft's winning in the Senate race. When Taft ran he won by 17,000 votes, approximately the number of votes delivered by Rabbi Silver's area of influence.

This was politicking I could understand from my apprenticeship with Governor Curley. I had not lost my interest in politics, and my work with the Palestine Committee gave me ample time to remain involved. The Committee's paper work kept me based in Philadelphia, but my lecturing, pamphleteering, and proselytizing the Zionist cause wherever I was invited to do so, took me up and down the northeast coast. As a matter of fact, in 1944 it was suggested that I run for Congress from the 4th District in Massachusetts, and I declared my candidacy, but withdrew my name when the party decided a war veteran would be a better choice

at that time. The candidate who was selected was Harold Dono-
hue, and he not only won big, but was to find a place in history
as a member of the Rodino Committee that sat in judgment of
Richard Nixon.

One day I found myself in Springfield, Massachusetts in time
to accept an invitation to join the entourage on Franklin Delano
Roosevelt's train taking him to Boston. One of the highlights of
my political involvement was that particularly spectacular day
when I was ushered, along with Orson Welles and others, to meet
the President in his private car. For me it confirmed for all time
the stories I had heard about his magnetic personality. It has been
argued that the office of President automatically endows the in-
cumbent with a glow of power adding to his natural charisma.
Perhaps. But that day in 1944 I was looking at a man who was
literally sick unto death. He was tired, old, and worn and would
die a few months after his re-election to a fourth term, yet he lit
up the area with his personality and presence. I wore a tie that
had "Roosevelt" embroidered across it, and that intrigued him
enormously. He chatted, had a personal word for everyone there,
and missed nothing of what went on around him.

That night I remember sitting in Fenway Park in Boston. The
large field was lit up by klieg lights. The President's car was driven
up a ramp and brought to a stop in front of a large bank of
microphones placed so that he did not have to get out of his car
to speak. His first remark was, "I have had a glorious day in New
England," and it seemed to me the sky would split open with the
cannonading cheer that rose up from the packed stadium. That
was the night he went on to speak about that "cabal" of congress-
men that had been responsible for so many of his congressional
problems, "Martin, Barton, and Fish." The crowd roared its
approval, and a footnote to history was born. A team was later
organized to go around the state of Massachusetts to present the

case for the Democratic ticket, and John Morrow, chairman of the party, asked me to represent the President. I was to do so for the following months until the election.

The incident I remember most fondly occurred the day after the Fenway Park rally. Congressman Joe Casey of Clinton came to me that evening at the hotel headquarters to ask a favor. "Stanley, you know that the bunch of us are all Catholics. This senator, Harry Truman, running for vice-president, is going to need someone to escort him to church tomorrow. He's a very religious man. As our resident Protestant, you're it." The next morning I presented myself at Senator Truman's hotel door, was met by Matt Connolly, his secretary, and announced I had come to escort the Senator to church. As Mr. Truman and I walked across the Boston Common we talked and I found him a very unpretentious, gracious, smiling, affectionate man over whom I towered physically. We were to spend most of that day together sharing several platforms delivering speeches. It was his custom not to speak politically on a Sunday. He would instead deliver homilies about morality, Christianity, and the virtues of the American way.

That evening back at headquarters John Morrow asked about Senator Truman and what kind of day I spent. I reported that I had found the man delightful and that all day, in the back of my mind, was the thought that I was with the man who would be the next President of the United States should we win the election. It was no secret even then, that F.D.R. was too ill to really be expected to fulfill the four years if he won. John Morrow looked at me momentarily and then made the remark that was to be repeated all over the country by political experts, "God forbid that Harry Truman should ever become President." That was not a remark in hopes for F.D.R.'s good health, but from the conviction that Harry Truman would not know what to do with the country if he ran it. Chalk up another failure for political acumen.

FROM PULPIT TO POLITICS

That January I was to be one of the twenty-six hundred guests invited to attend the inauguration. I was very proud to go to the White House that day. The ceremonies were held out of doors with the President taking the oath of office from the balcony at the rear of the White House. We stood in a gentle snowfall and heard the President sworn in for an historic, unprecedented fourth term. In a few days he would go to Yalta. In a few months he would be coming home to die. The night of the inauguration I went to the Thousand Dollar Club dinner for people who had donated toward the inaugural expenses. Obviously my ticket was free. At that dinner I heard George Jessel make reference to a luncheon once held for fifteen hundred people in the White House. Jessel remarked that the menu reminded him of a mountaineer who was asked what his hash was composed of, and he replied, "horse and rabbit, one horse and one rabbit." Jessel turned to Mrs. Roosevelt and said, "This afternoon at the White House lunch you served chicken salad. One chicken and fifteen hundred bunches of celery." In her own gentle, giggly way, Mrs. Roosevelt responded ambiguously, I thought, "Mr. Jessel, you were quite lucky to get even the celery." I sat at a table with Edward G. Robinson and Milton Berle, whom I got to know better later on through his sister Rosalyn, who became a close friend. The President, who could not attend the dinner, was represented by Vice-President Harry Truman, General George Marshall, and Perle Mesta. During my life I have been fortunate to be among people who were and are making history, as well as people of significance in the arts and sciences. Thank God, I have never lost my capacity to be awed when I felt it was justified.

On the campaign trails from time to time I would run into Jack Kennedy. I recall one meeting in particular when I thought he looked unusually tired, and I mentioned it. He answered, "I'm having a terrible time. Something is wrong with my back." We switched places on the agenda of the meeting we were attending so he could speak ahead of me and get home early. I had occasion to remember that incident in 1951 when I was living in New York City. Like the rest of the country I was glued to the T.V. set watching the McCarthy hearings and getting more furious by the minute. I am not quite sure which one of the disgraceful confrontations it was, but McCarthy was out after someone on attorney Joe Welch's staff, and carrying on in the usual raucous, insulting, tasteless McCarthy manner. In complete anger I rushed to the phone and called Kennedy's office. I do not recall who answered, but I got through to someone of importance and said, "If you don't do something about this guy McCarthy or get Jack to do something, so help me, I swear I'll go home and campaign against him when he runs again." The response was, "He's in the hospital having his back operated on."

When Kennedy was elected president, I was invited to the inauguration. I regret now not having gone since I was to Roosevelt's and Truman's inaugurals, but by then I was spending ninety-nine percent of my time working through various agencies for Israel and was not free to attend. I clearly remember the day he died. I was asleep, and the phone woke me. A voice at the other end said, "We've decided to go ahead with the meeting on Sunday." I asked, "What are you talking about? I spoke this morning to the people in charge, and there was no mention of cancellation." Silence, then, "Don't you know that President Kennedy has been assassinated?" I sat there in shock with the phone clutched in my hand. A friend walked in and put the phone back in its cradle. He had just come to visit because he knew how I felt about the President, and the high hopes I had for his administration and all it would mean to the country. I know it is fashionable to believe that Camelot was all charisma and no substance. I do not believe it but of course I will never be able to prove it.

My political involvement died down considerably but I did

volunteer my services for one more campaign. When Adlai Stevenson was running for President, I was on a platform with Governor Curley, and I addressed a restless crowd while we waited for Stevenson. Later, I asked Curley what he thought of our candidate, and he answered, "Stevenson was Woodrow Wilson, F.D.R., and Thomas Jefferson all rolled into one," I am certain there is not a thinking citizen alive today who has not tried to visualize the state of our country and the world had Stevenson been elected President instead of an ineffectual Eisenhower. A futile exercise in political daydreaming, but a fascinating one.

CHAPTER 4

FINDING MY NICHE

One day, somewhere late in 1944 or early '45, I had the opportunity to attend my first Zionist conference, which was held in Princeton, N.J. The conference had a profound impact upon me. I was still very ignorant on the subject and barely understood the ins and outs of the Zionist movement, but you did not have to be well informed to feel the excitement as well as the undercurrent of apprehension. A distinguished rabbi, Stephen Wise, reported that at least seven hundred thousand Jews had been murdered by Hitler. Had he reported the figure anywhere near six million, he would have been carted away as demented. Part of the anxiety at the conference was in hearing the horrible stories of persecution and murder coming out of Europe and not knowing how much to accept.

For me the most electrifying portion of that conference was when David Ben Gurion spoke. His observations, his projections for the future, all struck a responsive chord and I did not need the hindsight of the present to know that this was a remarkable man burning with a life-long dream and working toward its fulfillment. Even when I did not fully grasp the issues, partially obscured by his accent, I caught the nuances and for the time being it was enough. Later on I was introduced to Ben Gurion and sat around among others just listening to him. I caught an occasional reference to the Haganah, but it had no particular significance for me at the time. After the galvanizing excitement of the conference, my paper chores and rounds of teas looked even less inviting than before. I was still searching for my own arena of action.

Perhaps it was my discontent that made me notice the activities of others, but when I returned to Philadelphia, I began to be aware of the stream of young men going in and out of the next office. I have always exercised more than my share of curiosity, nurtured through the years by the fact that people hesitate to punch a clergyman in the nose. I went into the office and asked the man there, who introduced himself as Bucky Karmatz, what business he was in. He said he was interviewing counselors for a camp. "If those tough looking guys were counselors, I'd like to meet the campers," was my response. Bucky invited me for lunch, which in this case meant sandwiches at his desk, and we talked. I found he had been informed about my work next door, even if I had not been told about his. He was running a recruiting office for the Haganah here in the States.

During the early 1920's Jewish settlements in Palestine began to set up their own defenses against Arab raiders. It consisted of men from the settlements, determination, inexperience and inadequate arms, but it was the best that could be done. Palestine, then governed by the British as mandated by the League of Nations, already carried within it all the seeds of today's Middle East conflict. The British role was to govern and keep the peace according equal treatment to Arabs and Jews. The British, however, were politically allied to the Arabs and looked away during sporadic, bloody incursions against Jewish settlers. The Haganah (self defense) was organized in the 1930's as an underground force because the British would not permit settlers to arm themselves against Arab attacks. As a result, by 1936 Haganah was accumulating illegal weapons. At the same time, in 1936, England sent General Orde Wingate to Palestine as an intelligence officer. Wingate, an Arabist and fluent in Arabic, was also an Old Testament fundamentalist, puritan Protestant, and only a few months after his arrival in Palestine he became an ardent Zionist. The British government, by then conceding the need for a Jewish defense force, under British domination, to be used against the stepped up activities of Arab terrorists, asked Wingate to organize one. Using the already available structure of the Haganah, Wingate built up a capable fighting force. In 1939 General Wingate was returned to England because, according to official records, his Zionist sympathies became too strong.

When World War II broke, the Arabs allied themselves with Hitler. The Jews, always unhappy with British rule in Palestine, put aside their political differences and fought with the British against the common enemy. The Jewish Legion was crucial in helping the British defeat Rommel and drive the Nazis out of Africa. As a reward after the war, the British again favored the Arabs and tried to disband the Haganah, which promptly went underground again to emerge as the State of Israel's legal defense force. I have always regarded it as one of history's justifiable ironies that England forgave the Arabs for their collaboration with the Nazis but lost their Arab empire anyway.

Between the end of the war in 1945 and statehood in 1948, the Haganah was occupied with smuggling Jewish refugees from Europe into Palestine. It amazes me that so little is remembered about those illegal ships. Due to the Uris book and movie, *Exodus*, which bore only a wisp of a resemblance to the real *Exodus*, very little is recalled about the rest of the sixty ships that made illegal voyages from 1939–45. There was a group called Mossad (organization), an arm of the Haganah, consisting of a handful of people responsible for directing underground operations to smuggle Jews out of Nazi countries. Getting out of a country was not too difficult. Sometimes one hundred people became invisible crossing a border just by the payment of a carton of American cigarettes. Earlier operations were concentrated on just getting refugees into receptive countries, but later the operation was to get to Palestine, since friendly countries found very friendly and legal reasons for refusing entry to refugees.

There were so many tragic episodes. Most of the ships were unseaworthy and all of them overloaded. The *Struma,* with seven hundred and sixty-nine Roumanian Jews aboard, was fleeing from Turkey, but the Nazi representative Franz Von Papen was in Turkey at the time so the Jews were turned back. The *Struma* finally sank in the Black Sea, all hands but one drowned. Today in Bucharest there is a memorial listing the names of all who died. Next to that memorial is another memorial. A large, carved, marble book under which is buried five thousand cakes of soap made from the fat of a portion of the Jewish community of Bucharest. Memorials are always being raised to dead Jews somewhere in the world, but by other Jews, rarely by governments. Governments always manage to turn up as representatives to the dedications. That way they can still maintain a position of nonalignment. I can recall one exception. The Russians put up a memorial at Babi Yar, upon which the inscription refers to dead Russians. In Russia, alive you are a despised Jew, dead you may become a Russian hero.

Another ship, the *Patria,* also came to a tragic end. She came to Haifa harbor in Palestine with nineteen hundred refugees and to prevent the British from turning her back, the members of the Mossad on board decided to blow up the ship so that the refugees would have to be allowed to go ashore. Tragically, the explosive charge was too large and 24 Jews and 12 British policemen died, while many more were injured. The survivors wound up in a

British detention camp. Two young Jews, watching the ship's arrival from Mt. Carmel, were horrified by the explosion, and in anger and retaliation they planned and executed the assassination of Lord Moyne, British representative in Cairo. I must say that nothing positive was accomplished beyond creating a few questionable heroes on both sides. The British were as unconcerned about the assassination then as governments seem to be about terrorist activities today. They seem to serve only as a peg upon which to hang political exacerbations, in this case against the Palestinian Jews.

Ships continued to be bought, many of them fishing vessels and whatever old hulk was available in a harbor. They were repaired with immense labor, ingenuity, and insufficient funds, and sailed with fervent prayers. Not only were the ships used for an illegal purpose, but during 1945–48 the flags under which they sailed were equally questionable. They were secured with bribes in Panama and Honduras, and the papers for the crews were not able to stand too much scrutiny either. After 1945 and the end of the war, efforts were directed at taking Jewish refugees, especially orphans, out of Europe to Palestine. Refugees could not be expected to go back to countries that persecuted them, but they would be welcomed and needed in the new Jewish state that was anticipated, if not immediately, then soon.

The plan was simply to break the British blockade by running the ships into Palestine's harbors and landing the passengers illegally. Actually the landings were quite simple once we hit shore. Hundreds of legally resident Jews would leave their identity cards home and wade into the water to meet the refugees wading ashore. The British could not tell the wet residents from the wet aliens, and the ploy worked because of the sheer frustration of the disorganized authorities. Any refugees who were caught would be interned in camps on Cyprus. There was a time when internment was on Mauritius, but the conditions of the imprisonment were so horrible, there was a public outcry. By today's standards the clamor was small, but it was enough to embarrass the British into making a change.

Ships sailed from many ports, but by and large they came from Southern France with most coming from Bari, Italy. The Italians, even during the Mussolini and Hitler period were not hard on Jews. A large part of the responsibility for the Jews suffering in Italy could be laid at the doors of the Vatican and the Italian political leadership. While the political leadership was affected by all the ills and corruptions of wartime, the Vatican simply abdicated its moral leadership with the shining exception of Cardinal Roncalli who later became Pope John XXIII. Even today in the United States, I have found that any efforts to raise money for Israel from the non-Jewish community will result in ninety percent of the response coming from the Italian community. In any case, operating in Italy right after the war was comparatively easy. With the entire system being so inefficient, a few dollars would buy whatever was needed.

Next to the *Exodus, '47*, the only other voyage apt to be remembered by the public is probably the *St. Louis*, again due to a film more recently released, called the "Voyage of the Damned." That was the ship that sailed to Havana where the Cubans wanted half a million dollars per person to let the refugees land. The second stop was off the shores of Florida to wait, while in Washington a committee headed by Rabbi Stephen Wise pleaded with F.D.R. and Secretary of State Cordell Hull to permit the refugees to land. The decision was made that granting asylum to these people would be against the law, and the ship turned back. Twenty-five percent of the refugees were accepted by the British, the rest went to Belgium and the Netherlands. Both countries were to be invaded by the Nazis, and the Jews wound up in concentration camps. From 1946 on, I was involved with many of the ships, but the *Exodus, '47* changed the direction and focus of my life.

Talking to Bucky, I knew I had found my niche. I would join the Haganah, the underground, to become a part of that organization to rescue those who could be helped to leave Europe. I liked that affirmation of life after war. While working in Philadelphia, I spent a great deal of time at the Zionist Emergency Council headquarters in New York City. They had a speakers bureau, and the woman who headed it was a most remarkable person. As a young girl, Blanche Shepard had been one of the secretaries to Henrietta Szold, founder of Hadassah, then became secretary to Dr. Chaim Weizmann, who was to be the first president of Israel, and handled his affairs here in this country. She had arranged some of my speaking engagements, and it was through her that plans were made for me to meet Haganah representatives Teddy Kollek, Wellsley Aaron, and Danny Shind.

The first thing I had to do was clarify my draft status since the war was not over. I had a 4D classification, which meant as a clergyman I was draft exempt, but I chose to be re-classified and applied to my draft board for examination. While in the seminary, I had a bout with an ulcer and found a doctor who was kind enough to give me a letter testifying to an ulcer crater. During the examination I was found to have varicose veins. A psychiatrist who asked me lots of questions, some of which I found pretty silly, put down that I was suffering from mild anxieties. I found that pretty amusing since I assumed everyone going through one of those draft board lines would be expected to be suffering mild anxieties. I picked up my papers at the end of the line and found stamped across them "rejected." Inquiry produced the information that my varicosities were severe enough to keep me out of service, and I never knew I had them.

During my association with Haganah in New York, we used to

FINDING MY NICHE

meet every Friday night at a hotel run by a fellow named Barnett. If the Arabs who are so strongly committed to destroying Israel today were organized then, they could have destroyed a good part of the future Israeli leadership by blowing up the Hotel Fourteen dining room any Friday night. One bomb would have killed David Ben Gurion, Golda Meir, Teddy Kollek, Nachum Goldman, Meyer Weisgal, and many others who joined us from time to time. I look back with a great deal of affection on those Friday nights. I was studying Zionism at a night school with a superior faculty. We were presumed to be a group of people working on some sort of project, but in reality, no one individual really knew what the other was doing specifically. We knew that all the pieces would fit into one pattern ultimately. Much of what really went on in those days was never really revealed even in the books that claimed to tell all. Many people most closely involved were never interviewed and, if questioned, would not say what happened. One of the men who deserves a great deal of praise is Dewey Stone, from Brockton, Massachusetts, who was head of the operation in this country and pulled all the details together.

I discovered that with discretion I could continue to function as executive director of the American—Christian Palestine Committee in public, while in private I was moving around and meeting people on Zionist business as discreetly as possible. I was helping to raise funds to buy the guns, bullets, and ships needed for the creation of a new state. Bucky called me in one day and told me they had rounded up a great liner called the *President Garfield*. This was the ship the Haganah would take to Europe to pick up refugees for Palestine. With the understanding that every step of this operation from the loading of the refugees to the landing in Palestine would be opposed by the British and would have to be accomplished with as much secrecy as possible, I made my decision to join the crew. It would be a matter of some months before I would discover the ship was not the Garfield but the Warfield, a ship named after the owner of the Baltimore Bay Line and the uncle of Wallace Warfield Simpson, wife of the Duke of Windsor. This was the ship that would be known historically as the *Exodus, 1947.*

CHAPTER 5

S. S. WARFIELD

I arrived in Baltimore after having spent a few days in New York City in Harold Jaffer's apartment. This was a way station not only to break the journey for members of the Hagannah traveling through, but for briefings and rudimentary training where there was a need. I arrived by train with everything I would require in my duffle bag and met the bitter cold weather of this January, 1947. I went immediately to see the beautiful ocean liner, the *President Garfield*. What I saw was an old Bay Line steamer, the *President Warfield*, so far past her prime, that the thought of crossing the Atlantic on her seemed unthinkable. I had committed myself, however, so by the Grace of God and a touch of insanity, I passed from the world of Reverend John Stanley Grauel to John Grauel, ordinary seaman.

The *Warfield* was in disreputable condition as I soon found out. Boarded up on all sides, no heat, and infested with rot and rats, I had been told it had been sold as junk, and from the time the decision had been made to junk it, no one gave it even the most cursory of care. There were thousands of leaks and what the rats found to eat to keep them so fat and sassy was beyond me. It took the crew days of scrubbing, sanding, polishing, and mending just to make some order out of the chaos. Most of the crew were staying at the Lord Baltimore Hotel, which was the ultimate in luxury compared to staying on board the *Warfield*. Unfortunately, for the most part I was confined to the ship because I had been lecturing nationally for the last four years, and there was too much of a chance that someone would recognize me and create some curiosity about the ship.

During this period I was able to get acquainted with the crew. There were 43 men, about a third of whom were seamen, and others like myself, who had some measure of boating experience and a healthy respect for the sea. The rest were totally inexperienced but made up for it with dedication to a cause and abundant enthusiasm. Except for a few non-Jews picked up later on, the crew was all Jewish. When I first met them, I wondered how they would react to this gentile who was going all the way to Palestine with them. In turn I was a little disturbed about my own adjustment. Here I was projected into a society of men who had, I thought, a completely different approach to life. It was one thing to know Jews socially and superficially as I did, but we were going to be living together and depending upon each other as only men at sea do. Would I, by some irony of fate, find myself a persecuted minority? Would there be in the midst of this group someone who would be anti-gentile as much as some of my friends and associates at home were anti-Semitic?

My fears were proven foolish. As a matter of fact, the group was so diverse in its interests and conduct that I was often compelled to remind myself they were of common ethnic stock. Their reasons for going on the trip were as different as the men. The young fellow who wanted to get away from his wife. The young ex-fireman from Washington who was going to Palestine to join his bride. The ex-G.I.s who could not settle down and still thirsted for adventure. The idealist who was following a dream. The teenager who wanted to be a hero. The playwright, the poet, and the seaman to whom a job was a job. The psychologically maladjusted

S. S. WARFIELD

who did not know what they wanted, as well as the closely knit group of men whose sensibilities had been inflamed by the suffering of their brothers. These last wanted to become instruments of deliverance. At 29 I was the old man of the group, the odd man out. As I look back now at those six and a half months on the *Warfield-Exodus,* any little difficulties or differences I may have had with the men of the crew have long since faded in the admiration I now have for those men who wound up laboring on our mission with one thing in common: an intense love of freedom and an abiding respect for human dignity.

First there was Itzak (Ike) Aronowitz who became a close friend. He was a Palestinian, a seaman who had served in the British Merchant Marine. As chief mate of the ship, he would one day become its skipper. When the American captain delivered the ship to Marseille, he would return home leaving Ike to resume command from Marseille to Palestine, that part of the trip being in the hands of the Haganah exclusively. At twenty-three he looked about seventeen. Of all the men I have ever known, he was the most fearless, and throughout the months when there was a tough, dangerous job to do, he elected to do it. Even after he became skipper, he always worked alongside his men. Behind his back the crew referred to him as the "Little Corporal," and he could work without sleep when others who looked bigger and stronger were ready to drop from exhaustion. Ike later came to the United States as a foreigner and went to Georgetown University where Admiral McNulty was to write a letter reporting that Ike was probably the most outstanding student Georgetown University ever had in all its years of existence. Ike was of Russian-Polish background and brought to Israel as an infant, so he considered himself a sabra (native-born). After statehood was established he became an officer in the Israeli Merchant Marine.

The chief mate was Bernie Marks of Cincinnati, Ohio, who had been an officer in the United States Merchant Marine and had Master's papers. His knowledge of the sea for all of his twenty-four years could match that of a Master of forty years service. I believe to say that Bernie was born to the sea would not be an exaggeration. He was also invaluable because he was a veteran of the Haganah shipping operation, having been on two trips previous to ours. We spent many hours over a bottle of wine listening to his yarns and boisterous singing.

Next in command was Bill Bernstein, 23, from San Francisco, a graduate of the United States Merchant Marine Academy at Sands Point, and second mate on the *Warfield*. As a Marine officer he was in the Normandy invasion in WWII. Not especially committed to his Judaism, when the concentration camps were opened he was at Dachau and could not forget the obscenities he saw there. When he came home after the war he joined the operation to help bring the survivors of the concentration camps to Palestine. He did not regard it as a religious awakening so much as a blow for humanity. He was fond of a gag, at times a quiet philosopher, he sometimes preferred peeling potatoes and making up special stews to the headaches of navigation. He was to die tragically at the hands of the British when the trip was almost completed.

There were others. Bill Millman from Chelsea, Massachusetts who looked like a happy go lucky Boston Irishman and wound up carrying the scars of a British bullet on his jaw. He saw his buddy next to him killed on an aircraft carrier and came through the horrors of the war in the Pacific. He survived all that only to be wounded within the sight of Haifa Harbor by his former allies, the British. There was Cy Weinstein, physically large with a heart to match his size. Harry Leidner, radio operator, writing a play and brooding over the fate of his fellow Jews in Europe. Little Sam who stuttered when he got excited, but whose words gave evidence of deep thought and feelings.

The one who is closest to me today and a treasured friend is

Eli Kalm. Eli was the chief steward. When we first met on the ship he had just come out of the Army, and the Merchant Marine, which he joined because the depression prevented him from furthering his formal education, and he has been educating himself ever since. Born in Far Rockaway, New York City, into a very closely knit Jewish family he used to get long, chatty latters from them where they discussed every event including the menus at family parties. He shared those exciting letters with me and gave me a deeper understanding of Jewish family life. Eli still is one of those renaissance men whose interests vary from his passion for opera and baroque music, to baseball down to the last batting average. Deeply sensitive and committed to his people, I value his friendship highly.

I do not believe that in the history of the sea there was ever a crew with such a high level of taste in the arts, sciences, literature, and music. During off hours the crew's quarters and recreation lounge resounded with discussion and arguments worthy of the highest academies of learning. We had been presented with a phonograph and record library, and the ship's passages rang with the music of Bach, Beethoven, Bloch, and a host of others. Days were consumed discussing Picasso, Monet, Cezanne and Michelangelo among other works of art. Our poet in residence read his works to us to have them lavishly praised or analyzed to death. We talked of Judaism and Jesuits, existentialism and the Women's Christian Temperance Union, with Marxism, women and politics coming in for their share of attention. All of this while we were scrubbing, mending, polishing, and anxiously waiting to depart.

Every once in awhile I would cautiously wander into town in the company of other crew members to visit the cafes and bistros which mark every waterfront in the world. I was secretly amused at myself. Not so long ago, wearing my clericals, I had been running up and down the streets of a small town in Maine tending to the endless errands of a preacher. Now by a twist of fate I was dressed in a pair of jeans, a peacoat and bos'ns cap and was loafing in places of sin I and my church had so roundly condemned. Actually our pleasures were innocent enough. Cy had one consuming vice. He loved shooting galleries, and it was all we could do to drag him away from the determination to win two hundred dollars for shooting the ace out of a playing card with only three bullets. I think during the weeks we were stuck in port it took him almost that amount to find out he could not do it. We found a little shop on Charles Street back of a book store where you could have the most delicious elderberry wine, hot sausages, and black bread. A stringed orchestra entertained us with their interpretations of the classics. It was a wonderful place. We sat and argued by the fire expecting Mr. Pickwick to come through the door any minute. I was to see the counterpart of that shop a dozen times in Montmartre in Paris, but the fellowship of those days has fixed the Charles Street shop in my mind.

One day, as I was working somewhere or other on the ship, Ike came to me very much excited. He announced he had just come from a house of prostitution in Norfolk. I thought I knew what was coming next and was less than charmed because we had a limited amount of penicillin on board, and I did not want to expend any on the crew. I guessed wrong. Ike explained he met a Jewish girl there, named Anne, and she had gotten wind of our trip. She wanted to help, but aside from her willingness to run errands, she wanted to make a more meaningful contribution and sent us a recruit for the crew. He was a photographer and since we already had a good one, I did not see the need for another. However we were an all volunteer crew and could always use another deck hand. I agreed to support Ike in his request for the new recruit to join us. Anne's gift to us spent the entire trip across the Atlantic flat on his back with one the worst cases of seasickness I have ever seen, and little sympathy from the crew. So much for recruiting in brothels.

We were very fortunate in that we had the services, aid, and friendship of an excellent Baltimore physician, Dr. Herman Seidel, a general practitioner and leading Zionist. He checked out the health of the crew and gave us the vaccinations we would need for the trip. He used his contacts to collect money and pharmaceutical materials for use on the voyage and over the years recruited many young men for the Haganah. He knew what would be required for the problems we would encounter with forty-five hundred refugees on board including any births that might occur. He had everything assembled and brought on board after dark. In the same way and through other devoted Zionists, we outfitted the ship for every need we could possibly foresee, including thousands of cartons of cigarettes which would be invaluable in Europe both for sales when we needed money and bribes when we needed help. Since supplies for forty-five hundred cannot be explained in terms of a forty-three man crew, everything had to be crated and accounted for as cargo in case of a visit from U.S. customs.

About a week before we did sail a ceremony took place on board. The crew and some very important guests gathered as the crew took the Haganah oath. We were each given a sweater and a bible, *Old Testament* for everyone else, *New Testament* for me, which I regarded as very thoughtful. Ike was presented with the Haganah flag, now familiar as the flag of Israel, and a bottle of champagne to be used somewhere in the Mediterranean when the *Warfield* was given her Hebrew name. A few people were asked to say a few words and I thought, when asked, that this was the time to explain my own membership in the crew, which I did in terms of an incident during WWII. "Some soldiers were bivouacked somewhere in Italy, near a monastery. One Friday night they decided to hold Sabbath services in the monastery garden. To hold religious services Jews must have a minyan, that is, ten Jewish men. Having only nine, they looked around and spied a statue of Jesus and remembering He was Jewish, they held their services." A little later the party ended and we were back to our chores.

The weather continued to be cold, and snow blanketed everything in sight. The nights were long and miserable, particularly if you were on watch. We had some heat now, but it was restricted to living quarters and the mess. We stood watch at the end of a gangway where every blast of the wind made itself felt. The problem was partially solved by rigging up a chair with a kitchen hot plate under the seat. The trouble was that while one end of you was nicely toasted, every other part of you froze. Finally on February 25, 1947 we pulled up anchor and sailed, but we never took into account the perversity of nature so early in the trip. Only a few hours out, and we were hit by a storm that soon worked itself up to hurricane force.

We began to take water and found it was because no one had cemented the hawse pipes. Those are the openings through which the anchor chain runs to the anchor and after you up anchor those holes should be cemented closed. We tried to plug the holes with everything in sight that we could use, but it did not help. We attempted to start auxiliary pumps, but some problem arose there and we gave that up. The watertight doors were ordered closed, but in several hours the storerooms filled with several tons of water. Those of us who, like myself, still maintained their faith in the Almighty, took time out to say a prayer. While we were directing our S.O.S. upward, the Captain put in an S.O.S. for the Coast Guard, and the fight to keep the ship afloat began. The *Warfield* limped into Norfolk two days later, lucky to be afloat. I found out that we were one of nine ships in trouble during that storm, and one sank with a loss of many lives. The damage to our ship was repairable but it would take time and that commodity was in short supply for us. We had received word before we left that the displaced persons we were to take on to Palestine had already started to move toward our rendezvous point and en route thirty-nine had frozen to death in a freight car. With this bad news, we were prodded into working as hard as we humanly could.

Because of the storm, some of the crew who had never been to sea before, decided they were destined after all to be happy landlubbers. They left and were replaced. Captain William Schlegel, for a mixed bag of reasons that I never sorted out, left as well, and I was told later on he retired from shipping. Captain Vigo Thompson came aboard as captain and took us all the way to Marseille. We sailed under Honduran registry because according to maritime union rules, a ship under United States registry could not sail with an all volunteer crew. Some of the captains of Haganah ships did not always work out as we wished. They were chosen from a pool of unemployed captains in the States, and we occasionally found them very unsatisfactory, although they were always well paid before they returned home from France. Some were alcoholics and others made free with the ship's funds. One captain spent a good part of the ship's money on a monumental binge in the Azores. Another became so enraged in Marseille when he heard that Leo Durocher had been suspended by the Giants, that he went on a drunken tear and tried to beat up twelve Frenchmen in a bar. Sometimes, though, an all volunteer crew can help drive even a teetotaling captain to drink. I remember one incident. I had been elevated from the galley to the bridge in only a few weeks, which must have been the fastest promotion in maritime history. When the storm broke I was on the bridge handling the phone to the aft section. The captain turned to me and said, "Let go the spring line aft." I related the command by phone to the rear of the ship to hear a voice come back saying, "Mind your own damn business. We'll run our end of the ship, you run yours."

The storm brought too much unwanted attention to our presence. All along, the public had been told the *Warfield* had been sold and was being readied for a trip to Canton, China where she would resume her career as a river boat on the Yangtse River. I am sure some thought it strange we were going by way of Europe, but if necessary, we were prepared to come up with an explanation for that as well. So anxious were we to arouse as little curiosity as possible, that when we purchased our food from the ship chandler we simply told him the number of the crew and the expected length of the trip. We never told him to omit ham, bacon, and pork because it would surely arouse speculation and perhaps innocent gossip as well. In the Baltimore Jewish community, during our appeal for funds, very large contributors were invited to visit the ship but were sworn to secrecy.

After the storm three men were selected out of the Norfolk community to help us, again sworn to secrecy. When they arrived to assess the damage they were followed by a contingent of Hadassah ladies with sandwiches and coffee for all on board. Amusing as I find it now, it was less so when it happened. We knew we had the British to contend with, and they knew where we were, but we certainly did not care to thrust ourselves into the limelight as well. In any case, we never kidded ourselves into believing the British would ignore us once we left U.S. territorial waters. The only question for us was, what kind of tender loving care did they have in mind? Restocked and refurbished, March 29, 1947 we left port for Marseille.

CHAPTER 6

PRELUDE TO DISASTER

We were on our way. The weather held fair, things moved like clockwork, and there were periods of leisure. I caught up on my reading and filled in my diary from the scribbled notes I had kept during the hectic periods. Friday, April 5th dawned bright and clear, and in the manner of thousands of years of tradition, the crew prepared for the celebration of the Feast of Passover. The tables were set with linen cloths, the food prepared, and that evening we sat down together. Prayers were said, the traditional questions of the seder were asked and answered, and suddenly I found myself close to tears. The reader had recited the traditional words, "Next year in Jerusalem." Here I was, a country preacher, a Methodist seated aboard a rolling ship in mid-Atlantic with a group of Jewish chaverim (friends) in celebration of the self-same festival Jesus celebrated so many years before. What made the moment even more moving for me was that we were on our way as instruments of deliverance in assisting those of the second Exodus to return to their land, Eretz Israel.

Easter Sunday I rose at dawn only to discover it was raining. Several of the boys joined me with little remarks of sympathy because they knew how I had looked forward to the moment of sunrise Easter morning at sea. There was only a glimmer of light, but suddenly we could see a little bird circle the ship and fly away. This of course happens often at sea, but we preferred to see it as a good luck omen. I was extremely happy. I read the wonderful *Resurrection* story and sang Easter hymns to the waves. To my surprise I went down to a breakfast of eggs and the most succulent, enormous, magnificent piece of ham I had ever seen, prepared of course just for me. Later at lunch the boys served me a little pie marked with a cross in colored confection. I was deeply touched.

Several days later we sighted the Azores and put in at Ponta Del Gado on San Miguel Island. It was a beautiful place. The little town, centuries old, was one of the most picturesque I was to see on my travels, but there seemed to be terrible poverty. When I went ashore, just to amuse themselves, the crew cheered and had me piped ashore as they saluted. A policeman nearby asked me about my rank on board the ship. Kiddingly and carelessly I answered, "Political Commissar." As a result, for the few days I was there I was followed everywhere by mysterious figures wearing raincoats in the best Hitchcock tradition. I was even followed to church and studied over the top of a prayer book. I found it all very amusing but uncomfortable, and very happy to be there with friends and a means of departure.

We had to refuel the ship and found upon questioning oil sources that British pressure had been brought to bear on those who could have supplied us, making them afraid to deal with us. While we were in a bar on shore, a Norwegian skipper came over and inquired if we were from the "Jew ship." Long experience had taught the crew forbearance so we did not, as my instinct also dictated, haul off and poke him in the nose, which was fortunate because he led us to oil. Before W.W.II Germany had arranged with the consent of Portuguese Premier Salazar to build oil bunkers in the Azores. Shortly after the beginning of the war, England took over that oil, and when Germany lost the war, ownership of the bunkers became a matter of dispute between the two countries. The Norwegian captain informed us that there was a bunker right next to the pier at which we were anchored. God forbid that we should intrude in an argument between two countries. We took what we needed and left the Azores. We proceeded to Marseille where we were to remain in port until we cleaned up and restocked the ship.

One of the members of the Board of Directors of the American-Christian Palestine Committee was Guy Emory Shipler, editor of *The Churchman,* an independent Episcopal magazine. My good friend Dr. Carl Voss, Executive Director of the committee, contacted Shipler before I left home, and they created a job for me as foreign correspondent for *The Churchman* with the appropriate credentials. With that in hand, I left Marseille and flew to Paris to get a visa from the British Consulate to enter Palestine legally. That would make it possible for me to go ashore, should the crew of the *Warfield-Exodus* be caught and interned, which was always a possibility with Haganah ships. I would simply be regarded as having been aboard the ship as an observer and as such, not likely to be held with the others. Once on shore I would be available to make a full eyewitness report of the voyage.

Once in Paris I reported to the Haganah leadership I would be available to them, but first I would apply for my visa. I made several trips to get help from the American Consulate, and the best they could do was to tell me to stay out of that turbulent part of the world because I could get shot. I went to the British Consulate and made formal application for a Palestinian visa, but apparently they did not care whether or not I got shot, because all they did was take twenty-five hundred francs for cables. I told them I wanted to pick up the visa in Marseille, and their reply was a shrug of the shoulders.

While in Paris I worked with a truly exceptional woman, Shulamit, daughter of Chaim Arlossoroff who was assassinated in

1936 in Tel Aviv, allegedly by a man named Stavski. It was a political murder, and there is still disagreement as to Stavski's guilt or innocence, with prominent and responsible people on both sides of the issue. What added poignancy to the slaying was that Chaim Arlossoroff, like all underground people, carried all information in his head, not sharing his information with anyone. After his death, a plan for rescuing seventeen thousand Jewish children had to be abandoned because he had been the only one who knew the details and the contacts. Except for an occasional message on onionskin paper that could be folded up to the size of your thumb and chewed up if necessary, I also learned to rely on my memory. A good memory can be acquired by frequently exercising those faculties of your brain, and to this day I have almost total recall. I was with the Jewish Defense Ministry in Exile, which is about the only way to describe that facet of leadership, and I carried messages that could not be trusted to ordinary means of communication.

Shula and I worked together frequently, and I found her altogether remarkable. One of her responsibilities was to facilitate the passage of the children from displaced persons camps through the underground to the points of embarkation on our ships for the illegal landings in Palestine. She was unflappable, intelligent, and totally committed to her work. She slept and ate only when absolutely necessary and kept going almost to the point of exhaustion. She kept saying over and over again, "The children are our future." One day Shula came to tell me, with some amusement, that we had quite a coup. "You know how confused things are now," she said. "I am in contact with several agencies that work with refugees. Well, some area of the Catholic Church in America has collected funds to be used specifically for Catholic children dislocated by the war. I have been given those funds and have to decide what to do with them."

A day or two later she came back with her decision. "I know

where we can spend the money. Over twelve hundred Jewish children have been kept in monasteries and with private Catholic families in Prague. Now they have been released. Since they have been nurtured by Catholics, I guess it would be alright to spend Catholic funds to get those children to Palestine."

All over Europe, particularly in France, there were stories about Christian families hiding Jewish children. Some are legendary and have been made into films and books. There are incidents of Franciscan priests and nuns saving individual children. Instances like the Christian child that died in a convent, whom the sisters buried secretly and transferred her papers to a Jewish child. However, twelve hundred children are somewhat different. The only comparable incident was that of the Papal Nuncio in Turkey who saved a boatload of Jewish children by issuing them all Catholic certificates and having them moved from Turkey to Portugal. His name was Cardinal Roncalli, and I was to meet him years later in Rome after he had become Pope John XXIII. There have been efforts to destroy his image in the eyes of the Jewish community, but all one has to do is to compare him with popes that have come before and after him to recognize his great humanity. Pope Leo XIII refused to talk to Theodore Herzl, the father of Zionism, because he was a Jew. Pope John, however, in meeting a delegation of Jews greeted them with "I am Joseph, your brother." The last time I was in Rome, I went to the Vatican to visit his tomb. It was literally covered with flowers, silver objects, and tokens of all sorts. A few spaces away in the same area was the tomb of Pius XII. There was a single bouquet of roses in front of it which may well have been placed there by the authorities so that it would not look so bare by comparison. Pope John XXIII will, with time, grow in memory and stature.

Shula and I made arrangements for the transportation of twelve hundred children and though it was done through the underground apparatus it was accomplished legally because of the money available for bribes. For a few hundred dollars you could bring people over a border. Sometimes though, trickery was required instead of bribes. Once a convoy of trucks, curtains drawn, came to a British outpost. The driver of the first truck, a Haganah member in a military uniform, jumped off the truck, rushed up to the guard, scolded him for stopping the convoy, magnanimously agreed not to report him for dereliction of duty, inspected the guard's papers, (thereby confusing him even further) and drove across the border.

On another occasion in Libya a friend of mine, Wellsley Aaron, a Jewish major in the British armed forces, succeeded in driving off with quite a haul. He "borrowed" some British trucks from camp, loaded them up with "liberated" equipment, and got himself a motorcycle with a sidecar and a Jewish driver in a British uniform. They stopped at the boarder and Major Aaron said, "I'm moving some stuff, and the only help I have are these Jews from the Jewish Brigade. You know what they're like for God's sake, so don't hold me up or I'll be in the soup." The sergeant let him through. Everyone with Wellsley was Jewish, but he himself spoke clipped Oxfordian English and got away with it. Eventually the material was used in the first war against the Arabs in 1948.

Next to sex and toothpaste, the most utilized commodity in the world at that period in history was armaments. I knew a man in Marseille who would sell you five rifles for a bottle of American hair tonic because he had a particular passion for American hair tonic. The Haganah and the Syrians were being supplied with arms by the same sources, and we learned that the Syrians had a whole shipload of weapons in the Bari Harbor, Italy. The arms were destroyed before they could reach Damascus. Had the Syrians received them, the entire 1948 war with Israel might have had a different ending.

Some of the children Shula and I were moving were brought to Paris, but others were brought to Marseille where the underground had a chateau built by Napoleon, now being used as an orphan asylum for Jewish children. We had other estates in the south of France occupied as camps for the kids. To move the youngsters from place to place the underground had set up a string of travel agencies. The buses would pull up in front of an agency and disgorge its people onto the sidewalk where they would wait around for the next bus to take them to the next stop on this underground railroad. No one ever questioned the presence of a group of kids carrying suitcases and standing in front of a travel agency. We took them through the heart of Paris and after Israel came into being the shops remained open as legitimate travel agencies. Most of the children eventually wound up in Palestine, some crossing on the *Exodus,* some wound up interned in camps, or worse, returned to the lands of their worst nightmares.

British interest in us never waned. Shula and I were eating in a cafe in Marseille with a British agent dining in another corner of the room, just as he had eaten lunch with us every day for a week. He was so obvious, wearing a moustache, a tattersall jacket, and smoking a pipe. I think every British agent looked like a graduate from Sandringham, and they all wore the same outfits. It could all have been a scene out of a grade B late night movie on TV, but it was real. Sometimes we found the British very amusing—up to a point. The code word for the refugees aboard one of our ships, the *Hatikvah,* was "bananas," and just for the fun of it someone leaked the story that British Foreign Minister Ernest Bevin had broken the banana code and paralyzed the underground operation. It was front page news in the *London Observer*. It ceased to be fun when the British picked up newsman I.F. Stone and interrogated him for five hours because of a slip they found in his pocket.

"Come on, Mr. Stone. What does this mean, one pound of carrots, one head of cabbage, two pounds of sugar?" Stone said,

"It's nothing. I'm an American male. I went to the market for my wife before I left home and stuck her shopping list in my pocket." The British insisted, "Come on, Mr. Stone, this is ridiculous," and over and over again for five hours.

During 1947 I made many trips to Marseille to help move refugees or to act as a courier and found Marseille, unlike Paris, was home to many scurrilous characters. The free port of French Tangier hid about one third of the world's criminals in those years, and many of them drifted into Marseille to work at various nefarious occupations. I lived in a section that had been declared out of bounds to American soldiers because it was such a high crime area. Working with us were Spanish refugees from France, who could not go home while Franco was dictator. There were former members of the French Maquis who could not seem to go back to normal living, and an assortment of adventurers from everywhere who did not mind doing anything as long as they were well paid. I also got to know many Arabs who suspected that we were working for the Jewish underground, but they had interests of their own and could not care less.

While still in Paris, I got a hurried call from Shula to meet her at the Place de la Concorde because there was some trouble brewing. When we met she told me that a Rabbi Baruch Korff had been flying over Paris dropping leaflets in support of the projected Jewish state. That was the same Rabbi Korff who was later to become such a staunch supporter of Senator Joe McCarthy, and later of Richard Nixon, down to the last tear. The problem was that in addition to the leaflets, he was allegedly suspected of terrorist activities in London including sending explosive magnesium envelopes to Ernest Bevin, England's foreign secretary. The British, with French help, decided to root out all the Jewish underground operators in Paris. Shula had received word that they were looking for us, and while the police were shaking down every likely corner of Paris, nine of us were sitting all in one row at the Paris Opera listening to *Thais*. After the performance, we scattered and decided to go back to Marseille and rejoin the *Warfield*. In any case, Marseille was a better city for me to be in because we had better facilities when we had to run for cover. We had a clinic run by Jewish doctors who not only took care of any crew member who needed medical attention, but they could hide people for us as well. Many times when someone had to disappear for awhile he would wind up in the clinic bandaged beyond recognition, until things were quiet again.

The sooner I left Paris the better, so I decided to take the night train to Marseille. Typical of France then and now are the sudden strikes that can pop up at the most inconvenient times. This time there was a strike of service employees on the Wagon de Lit, and there was a great deal of confusion when the roomettes were assigned. I ended up sharing mine with a French colonel and a lady, strangers to each other as well as to me. I had not realized the French were that broadminded, but then I was just an American seaman on shore leave.

The strike meant there were no blankets or sheets, just bare mattresses. The colonel came prepared for the emergency, and had a package that contained an air mattress which he blew up, a couple of blankets, and a dressing gown beneath which he carefully undressed. The lady was not as well prepared, but she insisted on semi-undressing, I presume to keep her outer garments from creasing. It created problems for me, because wherever I looked in the small compartment there seemed to be a mirror making it difficult for me to avoid the minor striptease. That night while I lay on the bare mattress and froze, and the lady tossed in the opposite berth trying to keep warm under her coat, the damn French train whistles shrieked through the night, and I hated the warm comfortable colonel snoring his way to Marseille.

I arrived in Marseille to be told that the *Warfield* had already sailed, having had to make a quick getaway. The British had three destroyers off shore and were aware of everything we were doing on or off the ship. We had every reason to believe that they would do anything possible to prevent our reaching Palestine. With the hunt already in progress in Paris for members of the organization and the possibility of British intervention in our leaving, the Haganah leadership both ashore and on board decided the *Warfield* should head for Portovenere on the coast of Genoa before we outstayed our welcome in Marseille. I was told there was a ship in Port de Bouc, nearby, the *Hatikvah,* another ship belonging to our "company" on which I had sailed before. The *Warfield* was in a hurry to leave Portovenere and would wait for my arrival. Before leaving France, though, I had to pick up my visa, which was supposed to be waiting for me at the British consulate in Marseille. I enlisted the aid of two boys, Avi and Ari, to drive me to the consulate office before driving me to Port de Bouc to catch the *Hatikvah,* but first I changed to my more authoritative clerical clothes. I was very nervous when I arrived there, but the Consul greeted me genially with a "Hello, sir. We were expecting you." I picked up my visa and left as fast as possible for Port de Bouc. That was one visa the British would regret issuing.

I thought the *Warfield* was bad, but I had forgotten the shape the *Hatikvah* was in until we sailed. She was a tiny vessel that had to fit in too many berths and as a consequence, they had only a few feet of separation between them. The upper berth above me contained three hundred pounds of Yak Woodruff and since the berths were not too well constructed and sagged, I had generous portions of Yak's anatomy pressing down on me during the night. I got out my sleeping bag and spent the rest of the trip sleeping on deck. The eight days I spent on board were enjoyable, though, because of the interesting people I met. One in particular was outstanding. He was a big freckle-faced, red-headed Boston Irishman, who had studied law at Harvard and had written a thesis comparing the Irish fight for freedom and the Palestine problem.

PRELUDE TO DISASTER

There were other gentiles on board with him who shared his passion for freedom along with a fierce antipathy toward the British. Some weeks later Homer Bigart of the New York *Herald-Tribune* would report that a steamer, the *Hatikvah*, was seized by the British off the coast of Palestine, with a load of refugees on board. On its stack was painted a green shamrock with the words, "Ireland 1922" above a blue Star of David labelled, "Palestine 1947."

When we landed in Portovenere, Bernie Marks came over from the Warfield to pick me up in the dinghy. I asked him how things were going, and he told me the food was terrible and the crew was complaining. Eli Kalm was chief steward in charge of the mess—no pun intended—and he knew nothing about cooking. That was being done by a fellow named Abbott Lutz from Norfolk, Virginia and his only qualification for the job was a radio program during which he read recipes. I strode into the galley like a primadonna and took over with Eli hovering over me until we both got nervous. I finally told him to get the hell out of the galley and never come back, while I took over the cooking for about one hundred people. I, the traditional New Englander, weaned on mince pie, baked beans, brown bread, and clam chowder found myself in Italy wrestling with matzo balls and potato latkes. However, the Israelis insisted Americans were crazy because they served jelly with chicken. They had never seen cranberry sauce before.

Eli did furnish me with an assistant cook and two scullery boys. The "associate chef" was an Egyptian Jew with a dry sense of humor who spoke English with a French accent. We nicknamed him Abdul. The two boys were Mexican Jews who were going to Israel to settle there. One of them spoke Yiddish. In order to get an onion peeled I gave the order to Abdul in English, who transmitted it in Yiddish to one youngster, who then passed it on to the second in Spanish. I wonder if Oscar of the Waldorf ever had to do that? Abdul had some of the typical attitudes of the Arab. I asked him to stir up the fire on one occasion so that the potatoes would be cooked in time for dinner. He shrugged his shoulders replying, "So? They are not cooked for dinner? We eat them for supper." Once I found him looking out into space, brooding. I asked him what was wrong.

He said, "You know, I am stupid. I had a girlfriend in Egypt. I was in love with her. She went to Palestine to live and I wanted to go too. My mother and father objected and sent me to America to go to school. So, I ran away and joined the crew of this ship. Already it has taken me ten months to go ten thousand miles to get to my girl. I am thinking I am very stupid. If I had only run away from home in Egypt, for a few piastres and half an hour of my time I am in Palestine."

In a corner of the galley was a large can which was kept constantly filled by the continuous process of peeling potatoes. If anyone, from the captain down, visited the galley to chisel an extra treat, he was immediately put to work peeling potatoes. The potato barrel, like the New England pot bellied stove, was the center of the ship's conviviality.

Food was always disappearing and I could not find out how. We locked doors and hatches with a score of locks until my key chain looked like that of a head keeper in a mental institution. The greatest mystery of all was the one we called "The Case of the Missing Halvah." What made it such a cause celebre was that halvah is a particularly delectable candy loved by Middle-Easterners generally. We thought we had done an especially good job of hiding it in a locker that was impenetrable, but it was stolen despite all precautions. It was not until many years later long after the trip was over, that some of the kids confessed they had found an opening behind some pipes back of the food locker only large enough for a child or a very skinny man.

One night Harry Leidner and I were on the bridge when we

heard the sound of a ship moving in our area. Morning revealed an Italian gunboat, machine guns in an excellent position to give us a good raking, anchored directly across our bow. Closer inspection showed they were sitting on our anchors, either by design or accident, and we could not move. A small boat put out from the gunboat, and a young Italian officer came on board to explain to our captain that any attempt to move out on our part would cause them to fire upon us. A little judicious questioning convinced us this was a British inspired ploy. That was confirmed when one of the boys went ashore and brought back a copy of an Italian newspaper stating that the British authorities in Rome had taken steps in cooperation with the Italian authorities to prevent the sailing of an unnamed vessel, which was to be used to transport "escaping criminals and fascists." This kind of vile propaganda was used frequently in a most outrageous manner to tie in every isolated crime in Italy with the operations of our organization's efforts to move displaced persons out of Europe to Palestine. I was enraged to the point of tears many times by the lying statements of British officialdom in their undeclared war against the world's dispossessed.

While the Haganah leadership was wrestling with this problem, I took some time off for a little sightseeing which I expected would be a little less nervewracking. Although I had an Italian visa in my passport, there was no stamp to indicate when and where I had entered the country. The law required that one report to the police within three days of arrival. This, of course, I had not done. It turned out that though I showed my passport every time I registered at a hotel, my luck held. I finally arranged to secure a stamp indicating I had arrived at a certain port, on a certain date, aboard a certain ship, where the possibilities of checking back were very poor.

My trip carried me across the towering peaks of the Apennines to Milan where I spent an afternoon looking at the glories of the great Duomo and visited the sadly defaced painting of Leonardo da Vinci's *Last Supper.* Then I left for Rome, the Eternal City, the city of Michelangelo's *Sistine Chapel* and his overwhelming statue of *Moses,* giver of Divine Law, the foundation of Jewish and Christian morality. Rome, its streets filled with black marketeers and literally thousands upon thousands of beggars, many of them wizened little children, pinch-faced and hollow-eyed. It was small comfort to look upon the vast treasury within the Vatican and know that within shouting distance were those who were hungry. I enjoyed the evenings. The heat of summer had not yet set in, and I took long, solitary walks through ancient ruins.

I visited the Arch of Titus surrounded by decay and thought, "This ruin was erected to a man who was directly responsible for driving the Jewish people from their homeland. He is dust and all that remains are these stones. Yet the object of his wrath, the Hebrew Nation, lives. The very persecution of which he was an instrument served to weld that great people into such a force that nearly two thousand years of horrible, relentless, mindless persecution have not destroyed them. As a matter of fact, they have been reborn in this last and greatest of their sufferings. That rebirth signifies the ever-present chord of life and destiny which seems to run all through Judaic history. They spring from eternity and will remain until eternity."

One brilliant moonlit night I went out on the Appian Way and then retraced my steps into the city. I walked in my bare feet, not in any act of faith, but because my feet hurt, yet what more suitable way to travel over one of the holiest of roads? Over these roads had been carried the broken bodies of thousands of Christians and Jews to their burial places in the dank and musty catacombs. St. Sebastian, St. Cecilia, St. Peter, and St. Paul had traveled its worn surfaces. It was one of those nights when you feel at one with the universe.

I returned the next day to Portovenere and reality, to find that the *Warfield* was still blocked. The crew had been joined by a number of Palestinian Jews, members of the underground, who were to accompany us on the voyage. Even today I know only one by name, Jossi, who was to become the overall commander of the ship and with Ike as captain, would make all future decisions concerning the trip. Jossi was young but very experienced in Haganah undertakings. He had bested the British on more than one occasion, and no one knew better than he that the success of our voyage would be opposed every inch of the way.

On shore, underground activities continued, although the British had invalidated all Palestinian passports of those they even remotely suspected were involved with Haganah, making it very difficult for us to get around. In charge of Italian operations was a legendary woman, Ada Sereni, widow of Enzo Sereni who had been tortured to death by the Nazis when he made a parachute jump behind enemy lines in Czechoslovakia during the war. Enzo's father had been a physician to King Victor Emmanuel III. Ada's first cousin was an admiral in the Italian navy, a Jewish rarity. Between Enzo's background and hers, Ada had some excellent contacts in high places when needed. She might aptly have been referred to as the Godmother of the Italian Haganah, in her ability to command. I remember attending a meeting in Milan where we all sat around a table that could have been in a corporate board room. Ada sat at the head, a tiny, dark-haired woman about forty, engulfed and almost lost in a massive Florentine chair. A dozen or so Haganah people were meeting to discuss some future operation. Voices gradually rose to a shout, hands were gesturing in all directions, tempers flaring, then one quiet word "sheket" (shut up) from Ada and a room full of lions sheepishly settle down like lambs and the work went forward.

In view of the passport problem, the organization needed some method of transportation they could use freely and safely. Ada learned that Prince Pacelli, nephew of the Holy Father, Pope Pius

XII, had an old-fashioned touring car for sale. I recall it was large and very boxy, perhaps a Packard, and we purchased it through a third party, neglecting to remove the seal of the Vatican. While the British were looking for us we would drive sedately through towns and villages at will, saluted by the Carabinieri as soon as they spotted the seal. As a good Protestant and a minister, I was terribly tempted to lean out the window of the car and make the sign of the cross over the people so as not to disappoint them as I passed, but I resisted the urge with the help of those in the car with me, who were ready to clobber me if I tried.

We rode around in Italy wearing real British army uniforms with faked arm patches bearing the insignia HMJF, His Majesty's Jewish Forces, and picked up plenty of merchandise which we never wasted. We just detoured it to Palestine.

One day Ike returned from a trip ashore and called the crew together to ask for volunteers to assist in the loading of another refugee ship secreted nearby. Unfortunately, a driving rainstorm blew up, and it was decided that only Bernie and Ike should leave the ship because a serious storm required the presence of the entire crew. The wind howled, and the ship rocked all night keeping us busy. In the early morning Ike and Bernie came back, and I can still hear Ike's distinctively accented speech with its British overtones, as he told the story.

The ship was a very small one, and the trip was expected to be exceptionally tough, due to the overcrowding and poor facilities available. Only the hardiest young people were taken on board because only they would have the chance to survive the grueling trip. Just boarding the ship that night was hazardous, and the refugees were imperiled even as they were hauled in rubber boats by lines secured from ship to shore. Later, just before sailing time, a young man appeared with a baby in his arms. An argument developed as leaders reminded him he had been told the child must go on a later trip. Tears began to roll down the father's cheeks as he pleaded the child was his last and most precious possession on earth. They could not be separated. "The child is apt to die," he was told. "Better a dead child in Palestine, than a live one in Europe," was his answer. They were allowed to sail together. Sometime later we learned the child died en route.

We were now blocked in port for almost seven weeks. We would have made some effort to escape except for the problem of our anchors under the gunboat. All this time communiques were flying back and forth between us and Rome. Ike and I would put our heads together composing what we thought were heart-rending letters that could move mountains, but we could not move one gunboat. Our agents and friends behind the scene were using all sorts of legal appeals and pressures with the Italian admiralty with no results. We quoted international law reminding them we were all American citizens. No luck! Suddenly, without prior notice or explanation, the gunboat withdrew, and we immediately made a dash for it. As soon as we put some appreciable distance between us, the gunboat started to give chase for a day and a night, until during that night we doused the lights and managed to lose them. It was not until many weeks later that we were told Ada Sereni took advantage of her admiralty connections and forged a letter of release on our behalf. Today, Ada is living at Giv'at Brenner in an Israel to which she helped give life.

CHAPTER 7

EXODUS '47—THE BATTLE

In the very early hours of the morning two tugs met us, and the pilot guided us into a quay at Port de Bouc. Word was waiting that one hundred and seventy-two trucks had been roaring through the night with their human freight, and the first of the group was scheduled to arrive at 7:30 A.M. I had just bolted down one more cup of hot coffee when suddenly I heard the sound of the trucks. I rushed out of the wardroom to the aft deck where some of the crew were standing and looking out toward the concrete embankment as the canvas covered trucks rolled up, slowed, then stopped. The refugees climbed out cramped, bedraggled, and tired. A concrete stairway led down from the side of the embankment to a landing where a number of French gendarmes were standing at a small table with some officials who were holding long lists. The refugees began to move through showing their documents. We had moored a large barge alongside the ship so that it would be possible for them to climb the side ladder to board. They moved forward gradually, looking up at the ship, some of them somewhat mystified, I suppose. It had been indicated that they would be going on a great liner, and the three hundred and twenty foot Baltimore Bay steamer must not have looked very prestigious in their eyes. A little girl started up the ladder on to the side of the ship, and as she clambered over the top, I reached down to assist her. Under normal circumstances it would have been hard to distinguish her from any other girl her age, but as I reached for her left elbow, there on her arm I could see her number. The mark of the concentration camp. She smiled her thanks for my aid and walked on as I stood there, chilled by what I had seen on that child's arm.

All morning people were boarding, and we were assigning them to the few feet of space they would occupy for the trip. Soon the members of the Ha-shomer (Watchmen) arrived, and we furnished them with armbands bearing a red diamond insignia to indicate they were in charge of a particular part of the ship. They immediately started shepherding the people down below to get them settled. I asked Jossi how many we would finally have on board and heard his answer in total astonishment when he replied forty-five hundred. The ship was built to carry only six hundred under the best of conditions. As the sun rose higher, people came on board in greater numbers. They represented all the nations that had been caught in the teeth of the Nazi Juggernaut. There were some hundred or so Moroccans from North Africa. A few dozen from England whose accents were swallowed up in a babel of Yiddish, Hungarian, Roumanian, German, and Polish. There were the young, the old, the in-between, some in yarmulkes (skull caps), some in sport shirts, some elated and talkative, some timid and quiet, all exhausted. Eventually all found their positions aboard ship, and we made plans to sail.

Just as we were about ready to pull up anchors, word came to us that we would not be permitted to leave. The French authorities came aboard and reported that the ship would have to move up harbor behind the breakwater until some disposition was made for the future. We remembered the year before when the ship *Feda* had been imprisoned this way, creating a situation where Harold Laski, British Labor Secretary, had to fly to Portovenere in order to release the vessel, in spite of the protestations of Ernest Bevin, the British Foreign Secretary. At that time, the people on the *Feda* had agreed that ten of them would ascend to the deck at noon each day and commit suicide in the presence of the newspapermen, who had found their positions on top of cranes and other high structures, and were within reach of the *Feda* photographically if not physically. Bevin gave in to world public opinion and permitted the refugees to land in Palestine, but deducted their number, one thousand, from the yearly quota of fifteen hundred Jewish entrants. Years later at a meeting I met a woman who had been on the *Feda* as a child of twelve. She told me she had contracted diphtheria and there were those on board who wanted to throw her overboard to prevent an epidemic, but others intervened and sanity prevailed.

Jossi, Captain Ike, and a few of us in the crew consulted and decided that some of us should go ashore and appeal to the French authorities. I started down with a delegation of refugees who were to help us present our case, along with several members of the crew, but Ike felt it would be better that I remain on board. Should any problems arise and arrests result from the impromptu conference, it would jeopardize my future underground commitments by destroying my anonymity. We did not know then that the appeal would be useless because the French did not initiate the problem.

Meeting in Paris with the leadership of the French government, including Prime Minister Georges Bidault, was Ernest Bevin who had come from London to consult on what was later to be known as the Marshall Plan. In the midst of that meeting, an aide to Bevin came forward and whispered to him. In a rage, Bevin banged his fist on the table, glared at Bidault and told him he had just been informed that a ship called the *President War-field* was being loaded with refugees in Port Sette on the southern coast of France. He demanded that France stop the ship from sailing. For whatever reason, perhaps having to do with the present negotiations, Bidault agreed to comply with Bevin's demand. Neither statesman knew that one of our people was in the room and immediately sent word to our ship, but we received it too late. The port captain had already received his orders to stop us.

We were in a quandary. The refugees could not be returned to our collection points to await another ship because there was no way for us to take care of them for any length of time. Back to the Displaced Persons camps? Unthinkable! The day wore on as we discussed the problem up and down, inside and out, without coming to any decision. Then Jossi came to me and asked me to prepare a special feast for the French guards who had been placed on the quay to prevent us from taking any action during the night. A French-speaking member of our crew went ashore and invited the French soldiers and police to come aboard for a party. I set up a repast for them in the board room, and we were especially lavish with the brandy and American cigarettes. Late in the evening, after they had wined and dined abundantly, we loaded them down with pillow cases stuffed with American goodies, the likes of which they had not seen since before the war. That was the least we felt we could do for them, because if Jossi had planned properly, God willing, they might find themselves in a bit of trouble before the night was over. While they were enjoying themselves with us in the board room, one of our crew had swum ashore, cut the spring line which held the vessel aft, and the rest of the lines were recovered. As soon as the Frenchmen made the shore we started to sail. In a matter of minutes the ship ground to a halt, and we discovered that the severed spring line had tangled in the propeller. The tension on board now was unbearable. Then the engineer managed to turn the screws sufficiently to shake the line off and with a prayer we set off again. We made it. We were almost hysterical with delight, pounding each other on our backs with sheer relief and joy. Next stop Palestine.

GRAUEL

We were not out more than a few hours when we sighted a British Man-o'-War. To have arrived so quickly at the scene she must have been waiting for us. When we finally arrived in Palestine, we were being escorted by a British task force of six ships including the highly prized World War II heroine, the *Ajax*. There was even an occasional plane overhead, to make sure we were still around, I guess. Obviously someone in the British government or the admiralty was deathly afraid of an aging river boat overloaded with homeless, unarmed men, women, and children. Admiral Nelson must have been blushing in his grave at the new British enemy requiring such a display of force.

We were on our way and jubilant. We kept exclaiming to each other that we knew all the time things would work out, choosing to forget the despair each of us had felt in times of crisis. Captain Ike got on the loud speaker, announced the next stop would be Palestine and introduced himself, the members of the crew, and telling them about the Golach (priest) who was among them. As soon as we found some free time the first order of business was renaming the ship. We had been asked to come up with suggestions for headquarters, who would then wire their decision. All sorts of names were suggested, but the one that popped up most frequently was Franklin Delano Roosevelt. How our sages in heaven must have cried out in rage, but we mortals on board the ship did not yet know that F.D.R. had refused to order the railroad lines to the concentration camps be bombed, thereby condemning many thousands of Christians as well as Jews to be killed. In any event, headquarters in Palestine rejected our suggestions and wired back our new name, *Exodus, '47,* and I must confess I did not think too much of it at the time. A name that would make world news a scant eight days from now.

The days progressed on board and the ship became a hell afloat. The refugees were overflowing the ship and the sanitary facilities were woefully inadequate. Toilets consisted of holes in the floor

78

in groups of six, to be used by squatting over them, as Middle Easterners customarily did, but there were so few that hundreds had to line up to use them. Meals consisted of nothing but tremendous vats of soup, either potato or barley, served in buckets to be passed around, and canned pemmican, which we bought from U.S. surplus. Pemmican consists of nuts, raisins, and syrup, with sugar added, and was so high in protein and energy that the U.S. Navy required that it be part of the survival kit of every lifeboat. However, pemmican was to be eaten one spoonful a day, and I so instructed everyone. In spite of my warnings, the passengers ate a can a day with the result that most of them got diarrhea. The toilet facilities could not handle the waste, and literally up to our knees in excretion, we had to use pumps to clean up the areas. Added to all of that, the Mediterranean has a nasty swell, where waves rise and fall without cresting but creating a rhythmic motion for long periods of time and very conducive to seasickness.

The weather hovered around one hundred degrees Fahrenheit daily, there were no baths, and washing became a very cursory matter, if at all. The crew fared a little better on food, shared one shower and better toilet facilities, got very little sleep, and worked round the clock. I wound up sleeping in my clothes for the duration, lived on coffee and cigarettes during the last few days of the trip and over the span of the month lost thirty-five pounds. I also picked up a case of ringworm and a persistent case of trench mouth which I could not shake off for months until I got home to the States. These I generously shared with the passengers who gifted me with them originally. Along with the trench mouth, I had a skin fungus that defied treatment while I was in Israel. It was not until I was home and went to speak to a group in Ohio, stopping off to visit friends in Toledo that I was cured. Dr. Frank Epstein was a dermatologist in the South Pacific during the war and learned all about exotic skin diseases and cured me in twenty-four hours with an over the counter remedy he said was so old my grandmother could have used it. I sent loads of it to Israel to be used there. Thank God, I did not get lice. The refugees lived in such close quarters that everything contagious was shared by all.

There was little physical recreation on board for anyone, since space was a luxury. What we did was to furnish musical programs over the ship's loud speaker system and listened to the magnificent strains of the *Chorale* from *Beethoven's Ninth Symphony* or the lilting music of Hungarian peasant dances. In addition, there were frequent news broadcasts in four languages, English, Hebrew, Yiddish, and Hungarian, with copies of these broadcasts posted on bulletin boards throughout the ship for more leisurely examination. One member of the ship's crew had been a radio announcer and commentator, and he was extremely helpful arranging the technical details. Incidentally, many orthodox Jews will not speak Hebrew as a common tongue, since Hebrew is the language of the synagogue and therefore the language of God. As someone in Israel pointed out, when all your life you have used Hebrew only as a language of study and worship, it is very disconcerting, to some even blasphemous, to hear the language of God being used by a mother saying to her son, "Yakov, wipe your nose."

A child was born, both he and the mother weathering the experience well. It gave a lift to all on board. We were delighted when from time to time we heard spontaneous singing or laughter although it was difficult to fight the pervasive lethargy. Nights, a number of us would gather on the upper deck softly discussing numerous things to the background of the sway of the masts and the roll of the ship. Sometimes we would sing. If there were enough members of the crew present the songs would be American, but occasionally someone would sing one of the painful lieder which had found birth in the horrors of the concentration camps. One girl in particular, a Hungarian, was my favorite companion. She and her sister were the sole survivors of her family. They

1. HACANAH SHIP EXODUS
1947, Haifa port after battle at
sea.

2. *Aboard the* President Warfield
Baltimore, Md.
Left, Eli Kalm
Right, Bill Bernstein

3. *Refugees, carrying total worldly*
goods, boarding Exodus

4. *A wounded* Exodus *crew member. Potatoes in background placed there by kids who planned to use them against British soldiers.*

5. *A British soldier aboard the* Exodus *after the battle*

6. United Nations Observers dock-
side when Exodus limped into
port. Background: International
press kept as far away as possible
from refugees and crew by British police

7. Bill Bernstein being buried as a
hero. Haifa Cemetery

8. *Me with Eli Kalm, crew member and close friend, vacationing in Tel Aviv, 1949*

9. *During a visit to the home of Zipporah and Moshe Sharett*

10. *Me with Moshe Dayan. The bemused gentlemen in the middle unidentified*

11. *Left to right: Peter Jennings, broadcaster, me and James Hagerty, press secretary for Pres. Eisenhower, 1966*

Photographer, Emerich C. Gross

12. Top row: left to right, Rev. Dr. Carl Herman Voss and author Gerold Frank

Bottom row: left to right, me, Lillian Frank and Blanche Shepard

13. With two tremendously famous and talented gentlemen, Harry Belafonte and Ray Bolger

14. "To John Grauel
   with good wishes
      Eleanor Roosevelt" June 8,
   1953
            Photographer, Mike
      Zwerling, N. Y. C.

15. Mayor Teddy Kollek and me,
   Jerusalem
   Photographer, David Harris.

escaped to France where they joined a Jewish youth group and were now on their way to Palestine. I shall never forget her words when we discussed her future and I asked her what she expected to do in Palestine. "I shall be glad just to find a little happiness," she whispered. It is still a matter of pain to me now to know how many of that generation of youngsters grew up never having achieved that goal. Whenever I was free I would wander among the passengers with a word here and there, playing with the children, offering words of cheer where I could. To movie buffs, let me hasten to add that on the *Exodus* I never saw Paul Newman or Eva Marie Saint. The only visible love story I did see was the one shared by forty-five hundred people with Eretz Israel, Palestine, their Eternal Homeland. That love made the trip endurable.

Soon I was serving as a trouble shooter among the passengers. They came to me with their problems, their fears, and expecially their quarrels. It seemed reasonable to them that being gentile, I could be totally impartial in my decisions between a Hungarian and a Lithuanian, a German and a Pole, a Jewish wife and a Jewish husband. Once a committee came to see me because it was Friday night, the Sabbath, and they had been forbidden by Ike to light their Sabbath candles. I explained that I was sure God would understand the situation and forgive their omission under the circumstances. A fire on board, which was almost a certainty under the prevailing conditions, would only lead to forty-five hundred dead Jews to add to the destruction of the Holocaust. According to Halachah (Jewish Law) life is sacred. There was of course all kinds of illness on board, with life so squalid, but our biggest tragedy was a death. One of our passengers, a mother of two, died in childbirth and her son survived long enough to die in a British Military Hospital in Haifa. We held a burial at sea after our doctor informed us that in view of the extreme heat and the possibility that the woman had blood poisoning, postponing

81

burial for Palestine would be ill advised. A moving eulogy was delivered by Jossi:

"We are burying today at sea the first victim of this voyage. The way of Aliyah Beth (immigration) is strewn with thousands of dead. We add this one sadly to that list. No words can change the bitterness of this day, but the thing which gives us hope is that we know, we are convinced, that this is the only just way to carry on in these times. This way of burial with no marker and the fact that this woman died in childbirth is the very symbol of Exodus. Exactly as it was in the desert in the first Exodus, the way was strewn with the bodies of unknown Jews. The child who was born here will continue the task his mother was unable to complete. If there is any compensation at all for her husband and those too who mourn, it is that we shall build with added consecration in our ancient homeland; that there is greater courage within us to surmount those difficulties which remain before us."

Wherever we looked we could see the ubiquitous British. They never left us, dogging us all the way. I had been commissioned by Jossi to prepare some slicks, hiding places, in various parts of the ship. They were to be outfitted with blankets, flashlights, food, water, and buckets for sanitary purposes. Lots were drawn to determine which members of the crew would use these hiding places in case of British capture. Jossi had a price on his head and the British would be delighted to get him, and that went for Ike the captain of the ship as well. The Americans would fare better than the Palestinians, and I would be regarded as merely an observer—I hoped, so far as I knew, though I had been working with the underground since the end of the war and no one knew of my existence.

If the ship were to be captured and everyone taken off, it would remain in port guarded by British police and soldiers, while Palestinian Jews would be ordered to clean it up. The workmen arriving to do the job were never counted as they boarded the ship.

EXODUS '47—THE BATTLE

Through with the day's work, they would disembark carrying enormous parcels of refuse. The careless British guards would never notice there were more workmen leaving the ship than arrived in the morning. The men hidden in the slicks would leave two or three at a time and proceed to the Haifa theatre where the last nine seats on the left were always left empty for occupancy by members of the underground fleeing from the British police. When a seat was in use an usher would call his contact, and the occupant of the seat was hurried out of the theatre, supplied with an ID card, and permitted to melt into the community.

If you made a purchase in a store in Palestine, half of your change would be withheld. If you made no audible protest and merely exchanged glances with the clerk, your change would go into a bucket as a contribution for underground operations. Every man, woman, and child in the country was organized to help when needed. Every bicycle, every cart, every moving vehicle was registered with the Haganah. The illegal radio, Kol Israel, which used to keep changing its location in order to avoid detection, could mobilize a community with incredible speed and efficiency. Word of mouth, and telephone, could round up thirty thousand people to jam a beach when an illegal ship was expected, to confound the British by sheer numbers. Once when I was sitting in a cafe, carrying a gun I thought was well hidden, a waiter came over to me bearing a plate of whatever I had ordered, with a note on the plate reading, "Go to the men's room with your gun. Those are British agents at the next table on your right." Still today, in time of war or other emergencies, the country can be mobilized immediately in a remarkably short period of time, even when one takes into account its small size.

Jossi made arrangements for a broadcast to be made from the ship through the Haganah illegal radio facilities to the entire countryside. By now all of Palestine knew of our coming and our dubious race for safety or the possible confrontation ahead with a formidable representation of the British fleet. This would not be the first time for this dilemma, but heretofore the Haganah ships had been smaller with fewer refugees. This drama was being played out with a cast of forty-five hundred souls. We had prepared a light program for broadcast and rehearsed it beforehand. There would be a few speeches of greeting from some of the passengers and a choir of children singing Hebrew songs. It was an exciting interlude for the rest of the passengers as well.

For the final portion of the program Jossi asked me to add a short appeal directed to the United Nations Committee on Palestine, meeting in Kadimah House, Jerusalem. I gave the following statement:

"Gentlemen, at this time we request you, in assembly in Eretz Israel, that you appear to gather testimony from the forty-five hundred Jews who are coming to Palestine in a few hours aboard the *Exodus, 1947.* We remind you that no committee was called to witness the death of six million Jews in Europe. This is your opportunity to fulfill the requirements of your declared justice in these matters. Witness if you will the heartache, the sorrow, and the suffering and the utter brutality inflicted on our people by the British. They have acted as the Nazis have acted. They clubbed and shot down in cold blood our women and children. These British are imprisoning our people in the same types of camps on Cyprus as they suffered in Hitler's Europe.

You have declared yourselves to guarantee equal opportunity to all who seek freedom. Bear witness in truth to that declaration and hear our case now. We urge you to come and see our ship and to sit in judgment upon the British who we believe are doing the very thing that the United Nations has pledged itself to destroy."

The British were supplying some excitement for the crew as well, but we were not entertained. They were beginning to act rather boldly, butting in so close to us that we could see helmeted, armed marines lined up on deck. It was a deliberate show of strength, carrying an implicit threat that was not lost on us. Whatever was meant to happen would have to take place tomorrow. I had been without much sleep for several days, and knowing that the next day would be a momentous one in my life whatever the outcome, I would need to be alert. I decided to turn in after a stop in Bill Bernstein's cabin at his request. Bill gave me a handful of postcards he had failed to mail in Marseille, and some other personal articles, including a rosary that had been purchased in Rome for a Catholic friend. He asked me to leave these things for him at Haganah headquarters in Haifa in case he was arrested by the British. As I started to leave I noticed that he had taken a crayon and written on the white wall over his berth, "You are fighting men who fought beside you for freedom, and now are fighting for other men's freedom." I asked, "What is that?" Bill replied, "That's my little contribution to the British if we fail tomorrow." I left, picking my way through the sleeping refugees, passed through the hatch, and fell into my berth.

As tired as I was, I could not fall asleep. It had been a long and eventful day, and my mind kept churning over what may lie ahead. We had brought the ship in close to Damietta (where the Rosetta Stone was found) on the coast of Egypt where we might test the draft and calculate the ability of the British to follow us. Our intent was to move along the shores of Palestine until we came within four miles of the beach at Tel Aviv, turn sharply, and beach the vessel as high on the shore as possible. We would then start moving the passengers quickly with the help of some of the thirty thousand people expected to be waiting for us on shore. I have often since speculated that if many of those people were armed, as they probably would have been, and the British police and army tried to keep the refugees from landing, as they would have done, blood might have flowed so copiously in the streets of Tel Aviv that the State of Israel might never have come into being.

I must have dropped off into a deep sleep after all, because at about 2:30 A.M. the ship's whistle screamed a signal of distress, and I was jarred awake, slightly befuddled, as I groped for my shoes. I rushed out, snaking my path through the refugees who were beginning to pour on deck, to peer through the darkness beyond the edge of the ship. I had just reached the door to the bridge, when suddenly the night turned to day under the search-lights from the destroyers. A fleet of ships seemed to be running abreast of us as if they planned to converge on us at one point. My eyes were drawn upwards by the lights to see a mammoth poster which someone during the night had secured to the single smoke stack. On it was a picture of a woman holding a baby in her arms, a small child at her side, and an inscription which read, "England, this is your enemy." Through blasting whistles I could hear a destroyer addressing us, "We are going to arrest your ship. You are in territorial waters." The door of the bridge flew open and Ike, thoroughly enraged, his face pale, screamed through a megaphone, "You're a goddamned liar," and followed that up with a stream of choice abuse.

I looked toward the upper deck ahead of me and there stood a group of boys and girls between the ages of about thirteen to sixteen. They were standing at attention, their chins thrust forward defiantly, one fist tightly clenched, the other holding a potato someone must have filched from the galley. They were prepared to defend themselves with the only weapons they could lay their hands on. Watching them at that moment I felt a feeling of great pride and overwhelming emotion. There was a terrible ache in my throat, and I suppose I could have been called a romantic, or in today's vernacular, a sucker, but whatever else you may call me, I am a New Englander. I was born and nurtured with the precious milk of freedom. Not yet grown old or cynical, as I watched those youngsters I was momentarily bathed in the aura of Concord and Lexington, and all the words I had ever read about the birth of America and her fight for freedom took shape on board that ship. I knew, I just knew I was watching the rebirth of a nation.

I had little time to analyze my feelings. I ran through a passageway and climbed the ladder on the port side to the hurricane deck to take up a position directly midships. At that moment the destroyer rammed the ship, and we were all thrown to the deck. Tear gas grenades were flying and exploding all around me, and their acrid stench filled my lungs, and made my eyes sting and tear. I dragged myself to my feet. All around me people were groping and crawling in search of fresh air. There was surprisingly little panic, but a great deal of milling around in aimless shock, and children were either in tears, or worse, frozen with fear. I could not know then what I found out later. Four Marines had ripped open the door of the bridge, one with pistol firing, then together they clubbed our officers and drove them out. Bill Bernstein dropped with a crushed skull outside the companion way. Several of the boys dragged him into the captain's cabin, laying him in the berth, then crawled out of the cabin through the port to get back into the battle.

When I heard that Bill had been injured, I went into the chart room aft of the bridge where I was confronted by a British sailor wearing a gas mask. I yelled, "I'm an American correspondent. I must get into the captain's cabin. There's a man seriously injured in there." I heard a muffled response, "Get out or I'll kill you." He swung at me with his club, and I ducked falling backward through the port. Twice I came to the doorway in as many minutes to beg him to let me in. The last time he threatened me with his pistol so I withdrew, just as the ship rocked again under a second ramming. I made my way aft to the cabins which we had been using during the trip as the ship's hospital. It was unbeliev-able. Nat Nadler, a Brooklyn boy, was sitting in the corner holding his eye, his glasses having been broken by a club, his face covered with blood and his jaw sagging. All around me were lacerated skulls. Apparently the marines had been free with their clubs. One crew member was being held down as he was shouting his intention to get back to the fight. His head was a welter of bandages. He broke loose, and as I joined with others to run after him, I was stopped by one of the refugees yelling in Yiddish, "We have caught some English." I followed him to where a group of boys were holding four very young, terrified English lads, their faces pale with fear in the ghastly light. They had apparently been pushed around because one of them had a gash on his cheek. I ordered them taken to the f'c'sle where from the locker I gave them some cognac and cigarettes and in a duffle bag I found an old shirt that could be torn into strips for the lacerated cheek. I left them with two guards outside the door.

As I went forward the ship was rammed again and there was a shower of glass. I fell down and rolled under the supports of the life raft. It saved my life. The raft caught the full force of a bundle of tear gas grenades, and just such an impact had killed a boy on the *Theodore Herzl,* another refugee ship. The effects of my fall passed quickly, but I went searching for water to bathe my smart-ing eyes. In the galley I found every pipe burst, but on the stove there was plenty of lukewarm coffee. I carted it and a roll of cotton from a first aid box into the passageway where I had seen about twenty terror-stricken kids, eyes streaming from the tear gas. I enlisted one of them to help me as we swabbed the eyes of the rest of them with coffee.

What happened after that is just a mass of chaotic impressions, with things happening all over the ship at once. I heard the chatter of machine guns and ran into the forward companionway coming full tilt at half a dozen British sailors who were already in possession of that area of the ship. They trained their guns on me, and I said I was an American correspondent and one of them said, "I say, can't we stop this bloody mess?" At that moment a door flew open, and a refugee leaped in swinging a large fire axe. They held him at bay with their guns. There was much screaming by the refugees, but finally it was agreed that some sort of negotiations should be started for a truce, if a leader could be found to accept the responsibility. Jossi and others of the crew gathered to discuss a truce, and the first thing I asked for was a British doctor to go see Bill. The British ignored my request and informed us that unless we surrendered, they would ram us with their cruiser, the *Ajax*. We all knew the *Exodus* could not stand another ramming. An old man standing near me muttered, "I've survived the Czarist Russian pogroms, the Polish anti-Semites, and the Nazi murderers. With God's help, I'll survive the British, too."

In the meantime our radio operator contacted Kol Yisroel and sent the following messages as the battle progressed:

"Before dawn at about 2:30 A.M. this morning we were attacked suddenly and without warning by six destroyers and one cruiser. We were 17 miles from the shores of Palestine and in international waters. The assailants immediately opened fire, threw gas bombs, and rammed our ship from three directions. On deck there are one dead, five dying, twenty seriously wounded, and one hundred less seriously wounded."

"Under a hail of fire and gas bombs, the naval forces succeeded in boarding the vessel and seizing the bridge, but the ship's crew were not deterred. By using a reserve wheel in the hold of the ship, we succeeded in piloting the ship in the proper direction."

The resistance continued for three hours. The messages continued.

"Owing to severe losses and the condition of the ship which

was in danger of sinking, we were compelled to sail in the direction of Haifa in order to save forty-five hundred souls from drowning."

"The ship is leaking badly, and our pumps are working at full speed. We hope that if we reach the coast quickly we may save the ship."

By the time it was daylight, a number of British officers had joined in the consultation on the bridge. We requested the right, if we surrendered, to take the *Exodus,* in under her own power. One of the officers asked us if there was anyone present who could navigate. We did not at first realize, tired as we were, that this was a trick to find out who our captain was. Bernie Marks caught it though, stepped forward, and introduced himself as the captain and said he would take in the ship. Bernie knowingly endangered himself to save Ike, and the gesture would place him in a Haifa jail before the day was over.

As I look back, even without the expertise of hindsight, I feel that Jossi and Ike handled things magnificently from beginning to end. I feel now, as I felt then, that the British would not have hesitated to sink the ship if necessary, although I am sure Bevin & Co. would have regretted the resultant outcry from the civilized world. I cannot blame the naval officers who ran the various vessels involved. Their orders came from little old men in high places, safe and smug, sitting on their consciences in plush offices, and playing God. As to individual acts of terror, that is another matter. Most of those were perpetrated by young boys, and one of them at least, wept before the day was over and expressed the wish to go home. Many of them that I spoke to later on had a horribly distorted knowledge of the history of Palestine and hearing so many of the same answers to my questions made me suspect deliberately misinforming indoctrination.

I went to check on Bill Bernstein lying unconscious in the captain's cabin. Members of the crew were there weeping. Eli

EXODUS '47—THE BATTLE

Kalm stood watch over the poor, battered figure fighting for every breath. The British had finally assigned a medical attendant to stay with him. I took that opportunity to go below to the hospital cabin again to check on a fifteen year old boy, Hirsch Yacubovich, who had been shot through the head. The medical aid told me they could do nothing without blood plasma, and even as we were talking, the boy died. His brother, now alone in the world, came into the cabin and seeing the blanketed body, broke down in his grief. While we were there a young girl called from the hurricane deck that there were children who needed aid. There were bullet holes through their arms and chests. For the first time I realized that the machine guns I heard were more than scare tactics. They had apparently been used at random, regardless of the fact that the British knew there were women and children on board. On my blue and white armband, in addition to a small American flag, there were oil stains from the deck of the ship. As I reached for one of the children, blood spouted over the oil. Today that armband is framed on the wall of my study. Flag, blood and oil—a succinct portrait of Middle East Foreign Policy, yesterday, today —and tomorrow?

CHAPTER 8

ARREST, FLIGHT, AND THE UNITED NATIONS

The old, disabled ship steamed slowly into Haifa, nosed into place by several tugs. The young people, those still capable of standing, lined up on deck and sang *Hatikvah* (Hymn of Hope) with abundant emotion. Hundreds of British police and soldiers crowded the area. Cameramen took pictures while clinging to an overhead crane. Very much in evidence and obviously people of importance were two men, later identified as Judge Carl Sandstrom of Sweden, Chairman of the United Nations Special Committee On Palestine (UNSCOP) and the Committee representative from Czechoslovakia, Dr. Karel Lisicky. Soldiers in khaki uniforms and wearing red berets were lined up and at attention. They were members of the Sixth Airborne Division of His Majesty's Forces and had been trained for the particular job of "dealing with the Jews." I saw the British begin taking the wounded off the ship, and I ran back to the captain's cabin to check on Bill Bernstein to find that he had already been moved.

As I came out on the flying bridge, I noticed a stretcher being carried toward a tent at the end of the wharf. On it was the body of the boy who had died at least six hours ago, Hirsch Yacubovich, with the blanket down around his waist so it would appear as though he were still alive. I yelled, "That's the most goddamned despicable trick I have ever seen pulled." I would have fared better without the luxury of that emotional outburst, because all I succeeded in doing was calling attention to myself. The police demanded I come down and placed me under arrest. The *Exodus* with its overcrowding, plumbing problems, excessive heat, and poor washing facilities, made even marginal hygiene almost non-existent. We were probably the most fragrant vessel ever to ply the Mediterranean since the days of the British and American slave ships. The British officer who interrogated me never knew how fortunate he was, in that just before the ship docked I took a bath of sorts in the last remaining tub, in the chief engineer's cabin.

My stay at police headquarters was surprisingly brief. I presume I was placed under house arrest until they could decide what to do with me. They took all my papers, everything on my person except my money, announced I would be brought back to head-quarters the next morning at 11:30, and sent me off to the Savoy Hotel with two police guards to keep me from an attack of wanderlust during the night. When we got to the desk at the Savoy, the clerk looked at me, sized up the situation and told me, "There are American newsmen at the bar," and pointed to a doorway. I headed across the lobby and dove through the door before the police could decide to stop me. I had to tell the newsmen my story. British censorship in Palestine was tight, but with the U.N. representatives present the British had been forced to lift the news blackout. However, in the case of the arrival of the *Exodus,* they made news gathering as difficult as possible by pushing the reporters behind a barbed wire enclosure far away at the end of the wharf. Here was my opportunity to give the newsmen my story. The room was full of people, some of whom I knew, like Gerold Frank of the "Overseas News Service," a good friend with whom I had worked in New York, Homer Bigart of the *Herald-Tribune,* Clifton Daniels, then a reporter with the

GRAUEL

New York Times, Vic Bernstein of New York City's *P.M.*, and Art Holtzman representing *Radio News Service.* There was also Nat Barrow, *Chicago Tribune,* whom I did not know but remember so well for a rather nasty report he wrote commenting indignantly that the armband I was wearing had a United States flag on it which I permitted to become soiled.

I collapsed into the nearest chair and announced I was from the *Exodus* and would answer all questions. Immediately flash bulbs began to pop, and I was hemmed in all around by reporters. At that point with exhaustion threatening to overwhelm me and hunger beginning to make me feel a little light headed, I asked for a drink, thereby laying myself open to some reports that insinuated I staggered in and begged a drink. I was questioned at length, answering as freely and fully as I could. After awhile a reporter edged in closer to me on my right, whispered the Haganah code word for the day, and advised me to make my way to the men's room while the police were back at the doorway and could, at least for a minute or two, be prevented from following me. Waiting for me were Gerold Frank and Vic Bernstein who immediately rushed me out the back door and into a waiting car that bore American Press signs. It would only be a matter of time before the police sent out an alert for my capture, and we had to get out of Haifa as soon as possible.

Actually my crime was nebulous, and under normal circumstances I would not have taken off, but there was nothing normal about Palestine. I would certainly expect if it had not already occurred to them it soon would, that as a Christian minister and a witness to their crimes against the *Exodus,* they would not be overjoyed at my presence. Tensions and suspicions ran high during the best of times, and the arrival of the *Exodus* created additional strain between the British and the Jews. The battle at sea between the might of the British navy and the refugee ship, in addition to the presence of the United Nations representatives, combined to focus world attention on the British execution of its mandate in the Holy Land. The "United Nations Special Committee On Palestine" (UNSCOP) was on a fact finding mission investigating the mess in Palestine and had been ordered to come back to the U.N. with recommendations for a solution. The delegates, representing eleven nations, were traveling around through the Middle East listening, questioning, and accumulating information to help them determine what could be done with this area of constantly boiling nationalist aspirations and religious strife. The British were tired of their mandate because they could never control the area and would be happy to relinquish their burden if it could be done gracefully. I found out later on that my escape from the British had been planned by Teddy Kollek and the Haganah for the purpose of bringing my testimony before the Committee.

I crouched down in the back of the press car as we made our way through police lines and checkpoints. Palestine, always an armed camp, was especially swarming with police and soldiers on the alert when an illegal ship was expected. We headed for Mt. Carmel where we stopped at a hotel. I called the British Military Hospital and inquired about Bill Bernstein to learn that he had died. I was shocked and grieved and damned the bullying British for the needless waste of life. The sun that finally set on the British Empire sank a great deal faster with the sheer shame of the *Exodus* affair. We went on a few kilometers away to the home of the mayor of Haifa, David Hacohen and his wife Bracha Habas, a talented poetess and author, who maintained an underground hiding place for pursued Haganah people. This was the breather we needed just for a few hours while my nursemaids planned the next step. By then I think I was almost past caring I was so exhausted, and I am certain my adrenalin must have been on its last spurt.

We stayed only a few hours so that I could relax a little, then set off for Jerusalem where the Committee was housed and meeting at Kadimah House. The trip was nerve-wracking. The car radio was blasting away with a report of the *Exodus,* the police were looking for me, and we were going through roadblocks again. This time the roads were blocked by tanks, and it was very weird and frightening having the turrets stare at you and follow you as you move on. I still had no papers, but we were in luck. They simply looked very quickly at the credentials of the newsmen in the front seat and waved us on. Gerry told me when we were approaching Jerusalem, and I was thrilled at the sight of the Holy City. In those days the approach was around the bend, then straight ahead and suddenly you were right in the middle of the city. Today the suburbs have spread out and your approach is more gradual.

We arrived at the Eden Hotel and though my stay was top secret and no one was supposed to know I was in Jerusalem, let alone the hotel, within minutes of my arrival the lobby was jammed with people waiting to see me. They were all holding in their hands pictures of loved ones left in Europe, hoping I would recognize them as passengers on the *Exodus.* It was intensely moving. One woman with tears in her eyes said, "Shalom," pressed a package into my hands and vanished. She had given me a small silver dagger such as the ones commonly bought by tourists, and inscribed on it in faulty script were the words, "To remember the poor of the ship whose future is the hope, Hatikvah." I did not know then and I still do not know now, how they found me when the British police could not do it. We always knew what the British police were planning and doing however, because the man the Haganah assigned to protect me was also a member of the British secret service. He was Jewish, sophisticated, and only one of many double agents working for the Jewish Underground. The hotel was full of newsmen covering the U.N. meetings, and Vic Bernstein's roommate had gone to Lebanon on a story. As long as we were two in the room the police would not check further, and I could spend the night, but there was still one more stop to make before I could enjoy a complete state of collapse.

I was taken immediately to Kadimah House to the apartment of the Ambassador from Guatemala, Jorge Garcia-Granados. I was introduced as a Haganah volunteer from the *Exodus* and while I sat down to catch my breath, Sr. Garcia-Granados called Dr. Victor Hoo, assistant Secretary General of the United Nations who was also in Kadimah House, and an appointment was made for me to tell my story the next morning. I told the Guatemalan Ambassador about the voyage rather briefly and, I thought, rather badly. By then I had been without sleep for sixty hours and in recounting the trip I broke down from the delayed impact of the horrors and mention of Bill's assault by the British and his subsequent death. I had reached the limits of my emotional reserves. It was back to the hotel for me where I had a long, hot, luxurious bath and must have spent two hours just removing the grime and oil. It took weeks of bathing to remove the latrine smells of the ship from my nostrils. I slept on a real bed with a heavenly mattress and was awakened in the morning by Gerry Frank with a cup of coffee, a beverage without which I still cannot function.

After breakfast I kept my appointment to meet with the U.N. Committee members in Dr. Sandstrom's quarters in the presence of Dr. Hoo, Dr. Ralph Bunche, Dr. Garcia Robles, all members of the U.N. Secretariat, and Committee members Ivan Rand, Canada, Enrique Rodriquez Fabregat, Uruguay, and Nicolas Blom, Netherlands. They questioned me closely about my contention that we were not in territorial waters at the time the British attacked, and I assured them I had the ship's log to verify my statement. I gave them a full account of the battle emphasizing the fact that there was not a single weapon aboard our ship.

We had always made sure that passengers on the Haganah ships were unarmed so as not to precipitate any violence. Not only because ours was a life-saving mission, but because there was no question about the capacity for the virulent overreaction of the British counterattack. Professor Fabregat was very interested in children and when I told him we had about twelve hundred aboard he questioned me closely about them. Weeks later in their continuing investigation when the Committee went to see the *Exodus* refugees in their camps, they inspected the orphan's quarters. There Professor Fabregat saw a picture of the child that died, Hirsch Yacubovich, with a memorial candle burning in front of it. The Professor was so haunted by that picture and the children that he became a staunch supporter for ending the mandate.

I made one closing statement, "I have watched these people. I know what they are. And I tell you, the Jews in the European Displaced Persons camps insist on coming to Palestine, they will come to Palestine, and nothing short of open warfare and complete destruction will halt them." There was great gratification for me in knowing that my eyewitness report was now a matter of record. Inherent in the nature of the relationship between Christians and Jews was the fact that because I was a Christian, in this situation my testimony would be given greater credence than that of a Jewish crew member. I assume the supposition being that as a non-Jew I would be capable of clear non-partisanship, when in fact my emotional involvement was as total as that of any Jewish believer in the Zionist dream.

I was elated at having completed my mission and looked forward to my freedom to see the Holy City as a tourist, never having been to Jerusalem before. I had been assured by the Committee that as a testifying witness I was now under their protection and could no longer be detained by the British. Gerry Frank promised me I could do as I pleased after one more stop. He took me to an apartment house, told me to go up to the second floor and push the button, then left me. I did as I was told and Golda Meir answered the door. It was her apartment. A meeting was being held there of the entire Jewish Agency, the leadership of the Palestinian Jewish community, except for Ben Gurion who was seeing Dr. Chaim Weizmann off to Switzerland where Dr. Weizmann would undergo eye surgery. They asked me for a full detailed report of the *Exodus* trip from beginning to end and when I was finished, Golda was in tears. So was I, almost, and God knows how often I would continue to be, until I finally made peace with the entire episode. We all sat in silence for a few moments and then Moshe Sharett led me out on the balcony where we talked for two hours and began a close friendship that lasted until his death in 1965.

Sharett was a brilliant man who was fluent in seven or eight languages, and I think he understood the problems of Israel better than anyone else in the government. He had come from Russia to Palestine during the Turkish period and actually lived under the Turkish administration in an Arab village near Jerusalem. There is no doubt in my mind that had he lived he would have had a great influence on Israeli-Arab relations. He not only understood the Arab mind, but much of the Arab leadership trusted him. I remember asking him when there would be peace with the Arabs and he answered, "When you and I are dead, Jochanan." I am afraid he is right. The most outstanding thing about Sharett physically was that he could have doubled for Charlie Chaplin. In fact, someone gave him a Chaplin doll for his grandson and the boy looked at it and called it grandpa.

Though Sharett had been a prominent figure in Israeli government until his death, serving as Foreign Minister and Prime Minister, the Sharetts were very unassuming people never given to pomp or self-aggrandizement. I will never forget one trip abroad when I stopped on the way home to visit them. Zipporah, his wife, served coffee and cake, and I found the cake especially delicious and said so. The next day when I got to the plane to go home a cake was waiting for me and that night in New Jersey I enjoyed a cake baked for me by the wife of the Prime Minister of Israel. Typical of Sharett and his own attitude toward his importance was the time we got socked in at the airport in Montreal. There was a violent snowstorm in New York and we did not know how long we would be grounded. El Al passengers were all told to go to the airport restaurant where a steak dinner would be served. Sharett, not wanting dinner, ordered tea and toast from a snippy waiter who was in no hurry to fill the request. Finally, after an unnecessarily long wait, I called the waiter and said, "Would you bring the Prime Minister his tea and toast." In a few minutes we were surrounded by the maitre d' and a few waiters and Moshe was served. He leaned over the table and said to me, smiling "Jochanan, I want to thank you for using your influence on my behalf." That was a good crusher, and I deserved it.

During the Algerian crisis I had gone to Vienna, Paris, and Marseille at the request of the Jewish Agency to inspect the work being done to rescue Algerian Jews. When I returned to Paris I received word to go to London's Israeli Embassy. I walked into the office and was amazed to find Moshe Sharett sitting there. With no preamble or platitudes he said, "Jochanan, what am I going to do about *Perfidy?*" For those too young to remember that book, it was written by Ben Hecht, and a sensation at the time of publication. The book was a masterpiece of inaccuracies laced with dollops of truth, calculated to sound authoritative and impress the reader. Ben Hecht was a Zionist and a writer who was very pro-Irgun. Before Israeli statehood, during the period of illegal immigration, Hecht made an effort to rescue Jews from the Displaced Persons camps but would not work with the Haganah.

He lacked the proper organization and expertise and was doomed to failure. What he did manage to do was spend money and succeed in dividing the American Zionists with his diatribes. As a result of his rescue efforts and his vociferous public relations, he gave away so much information concerning underground routes and operations, that for four months Haganah operations had to come to a halt while we devised new plans.

In *Perfidy* he damned the Haganah leadership, Ben Gurion, and Moshe Sharett in particular, for their handling of the rescue missions. Having been involved myself I knew first hand how many untruths his book contained. For one thing, he referred to a letter from Henry Montor, then Executive Vice-President of the United Jewish Appeal, in which Mr. Montor had suggested that only young people should be taken on certain ships. Hecht immediately defined that to mean that the young were to be rescued and the old left to die. The truth was that the Haganah, short of funds as usual, was finding it difficult to buy decent ships for our operations. Consequently we were running Italian fishing boats in which the passengers would have to be battened down under the hatches for weeks at a time to fool the British patrols and only the young and healthy could survive the terrible quarters and the grueling heat. The older people were taken on more commodious vessels.

My answer to Sharett was to ignore *Perfidy* completely and not get himself embroiled in the whole brouhaha that went with it. I felt then and I still do, that Ben Hecht was an insignificant part of the Palestinian issue whose own efforts lent themselves more to the problem than the solutions. Even more difficult to justify to posterity will be the extremists of the time such as the Irgun and the Stern gang. I am not prepared to argue their contribution to statehood, but my own point of view has been that their undisciplined excesses have served more to muddy and bloody the

situation than to solve the problem. Even today in Israel, whatever your theory on the extremist groups, you will find an argument on either side at the drop of a yarmulke.

I continued to see Moshe Sharett over the years sometimes very
unexpectedly. There was one occasion when I spoke in the Waldorf Astoria for the movie and T.V. industry in New York City
on behalf of the United Jewish Appeal. There were many important and well-known people there like Harry Belafonte, Ray
Bolger, and a new celebrity I had not yet heard of myself, Ann-
Margret. From the back of the room, Moshe, then Israeli Prime
Minister, was escorted to the dais where he was being introduced
to Barney Balaban, Spyros Skouras, Sam Spiegel, and when they
got to me Moshe started to laugh, we embraced, he pulled up a
chair, I said, "How's Zipporah," he said, "She's fine." To the
startled UJA representative he said, "Sorry, but we both worked
together when we were shoe clerks." In 1965 he stopped in New
York City on his way home to Israel from Argentina and came
to see me. We spent the twenty or twenty-five minutes we had
together discussing the position of the Jews in South America,
and he never mentioned the fact that he was terminally ill with
cancer. He went home and died a few months later.

CHAPTER 9

GOING HOME

After my meeting at Golda Meir's apartment I was on my own. Loosely speaking that is. I was going home soon and until I left, the Shin Bet (Haganah's Secret Service then, Israel's Secret Service now) followed my car to keep an eye on me. It seemed to me that the British were following the Shin Bet and the Irgun (right wing group) was following the British. All I knew was that I went to see the Manger, traditionally the birthplace of Christ, and I could not manage five minutes of quiet contemplation I was hemmed in by so many people. Evenings were spent with friends in the garden of the hotel. Our host was usually the editor of the *Palestine Post*, Gershon Agron, formerly Agronsky, uncle of Martin Agronsky, television newsman. People would come and go, and one night I asked about a man who spent the entire evening with us without uttering one word. Gerry Frank said the inarticulate gentleman was called Aubrey Eban, from the Jewish Agency, later to be recognized as that superb orator at the United Nations representing Israel, Abba Eban.

Another very quiet and courteous man named Reverend Richard Zeisler always at my elbow for two days, was lucky not to have wound up lying in a back alley because for awhile the Shin Bet thought he was a British agent. When they found out he was a clergyman, they assumed I knew him from the American-Christian Palestine Committee. I in turn thought the Shin Bet allowed him to stay because as a Christian clergyman they wanted him to see for himself what was happening. It was not until I was asked about him that we realized neither of us knew why he was there. When questioned, he told us he wanted to find out first hand why I, a Christian clergyman would become so involved with the Jews. Several months later when I was back home I met Dick Zeisler, at his invitation, in a hotel in Columbus, Ohio. He was enduring a process of painful soul-searching. He had been born a Jew, and after conversion to the Episcopal faith he rose to canon of the Episcopal cathedral in Paris, France. We had a lengthy discussion about my commitment to the Methodist faith, and we analyzed the past, present, and possible future of the World Jewish community. At the end of our consultation he immediately placed a call to his bishop and left the church. To "atone for his sins" as he put it, he went to work for a number of years for the Jewish Agency.

Our delightful garden diversions in Jerusalem were also memorable, thanks to our hotel proprietor and his unique billing system. Towards evening we would often wind up with fifteen people at our table. We were each given individual bills, but also found each bill included the charges for the other fourteen diners. There was always confusion trying to figure out who owed what and inevitably we wound up overpaying, to the delight of our innkeeper. When night closed in we would have to go indoors because bullets would start to fly. There was constant sniping and firing and police patrols at every corner. I used to peer out through the steel shutters of my hotel room window and see them walking the deserted streets some distance away from each other so that if one was shot at the others could duck for safety. One night I was sitting in Gershon Agron's office at the paper when we heard considerable shooting, to be told later on that a nervous Arab policeman had fired in the dark at a British patrol, which caused sporadic exchanges all night long. The entire city was constantly so jumpy that people were shooting at everything that moved in the dark.

To further inflame a situation already found insupportable by the Jewish community, the British came up with one of their Solomonesque decisions. Cyprus camps being overcrowded, the *Exodus* refugees would be sent back to Germany to occupy the concentration camps from which they had been liberated by the war's end. With convoluted logic the compassionate upper echelon bureaucrats in charge of the fate of these Displaced Persons, I assume, must have decided that since the camps were now in British and American Zones, they would automatically become acceptable as residences. To compound this act of gross insensitivity, they could not even specify the length of the stay these poor, desolate people would have to put up with, since that would depend upon the yearly immigration quota for Palestine and the hospitality of other countries. The refugees, divided up into three ships, stopped in France enroute to Germany and were offered total care and asylum with full citizenship by the French government. Notwithstanding their pitiful condition, only a handful of people requiring hospitalization and medical attention, and their families accepted the offer. The others insisted they would remain on board until they were returned to Palestine. A British offer to land everyone in France by force was understandably refused by the authorities. When they arrived in Germany, which was about six dreary weeks after they left Haifa, many refugees disembarked in apathetic weariness. The rest of the passengers, still numbering a few thousand, had to be put off the ships, some dragged by soldiers, some hit with rubber truncheons, the rest gassed and hosed onto the land they had hoped never to step foot on again.

GRAUEL

So shocking were the total proceedings that witnesses who had lived through the horrors of the war were revolted by what they saw.

I was home in Massachusetts when the disposition of the refugees was finally made and the inhumanity of the solution left me with bitterness and a sense of frustration for myself and anguish for the victims. This was not what my friend Bill Bernstein and young Yacubovich gave their lives for, nor was it what the rest of us spent seven stinking months striving for. Over the years since 1947 there have been too numerous occasions for a resurgence of these same feelings: the Civil Rights murders and violence of the sixties, the Vietnam War and its excesses, the invasion of Czechoslavakia by the sanctimonious Russians, the unholy silence of the Christian community while civil war raged and still rages in Ireland, Lebanon, where the only plea for help for the Christians came from Israel; the "Boat People" as they have been called by the media, the Indo-Chinese refugees wandering the sea without rescue until Israel gave them asylum—and the list can go on and on. Will we ever see an end to inhumanity?

My stay in Palestine was a short nine days. I had been away from home for eight months and ready to return. I went to Bethlehem to buy some presents for my mother who was a little woman, but chunky, and made the mistake of letting an enormous Arab model the jacket for me that I finally bought for her. In spite of the proportions of the Arab, when my mother tried it on I realized the Arab had been missing some of my mother's fundamental features. The jacket never fit but went to a smaller member of the family. I also brought her some white damascene cloth which she loved and when she died the cloth was used for the covering of her casket. Buried with her were all of the things I had bought her from the Holy Land which she treasured. I remember bringing her a handful of seashells from the shores of the Galilee where they can be found by the millions. So precious

106

were they to her that she immediately bought a twenty-five dollar box in which to keep them.

As unhappy as the British were with my presence in Palestine, they seemed to make it as difficult as possible for me to leave. I was called in at one point because after my testimony before the Commission I had become sort of a hero and was recognized in the streets. The British were not happy about my testimony and being irritated by all the fuss that was being made over me, decided to let me leave. I was delighted. I had made two telephone calls to them asking their permission to go home since they had ordered me to stay after they released me the first time. Once they said in response to my call that they could not be concerned about me since they were not running a tourist agency. Finally I received a call to see Lieutenant Briance, who was second in command of the Jerusalem police. I made Gerry Frank go with me because I did not trust the police, and every time I did go to headquarters there were two men there. I did not like being outnumbered. One of the first questions Briance asked was how I got from Haifa to Jerusalem, "After all, we have one hundred and forty thousand soldiers and police in the country." I told him, "I don't mind telling you," and I could practically feel Gerry shrinking behind me. "I met an Arab who sold me a flying carpet." After a few more sentences to which Briance did not get satisfactory answers, he said I could go.

I could not wait to leave. The Criminal Investigation Building office where I was being questioned was completely surrounded by barbed wire, and you practically had to go through a maze to get in or out. I had been warned before going it would not be too safe to hang around. The word was out that one of the right wing groups was planning some retaliatory action involving that building, but my informant could not tell me just when. A few days later a truck stopped and a fifty gallon barrel filled with explosives on runners atop the truck, rolled off into a doorway and the whole side of the building including the interrogation offices was demolished. The rubble remained until the creation of the State of Israel because that was the British method of operation. When a building was destroyed, they simply left it and took over another one.

When Briance told me I could leave, he suggested I take TWA to Cairo and then home to the States. I went to see Reuven Shiloah who was head of Haganah secret operations and told him of Briance's suggestion. Reuven, who in the days before statehood bore the name Sezlani, told me to leave and return in half an hour. His report was, "You'd better not go to Cairo. If you do, the British there will pick you up and lose you somewhere permanently. There is an American ship, the Marine Carp, leaving for New York City in a few days. We will arrange for you to take that." I still had the five thousand dollars entrusted to me and Reuven told me to keep it, use what I needed to get home, and return the rest to the organization when I arrived in New York. The Marine Carp was a troop ship during the war and was kept in service for American nationals who wanted to leave Palestine. Although this was in July and no one knew there would be a declaration of partition in November, people who had no urgent reason to stay were packing up and leaving the turmoil and uncertainty. The air was thick with rumor, speculation, and fear, and with those who were particularly knowledgeable, a sense that some sort of explosion was on the way. Arab and Jewish extremists were out of control, skirmishes were erupting like little volcanic pockets all over the territory, and the British were ineffectual.

Even at the moment of embarkation I had a last hassle with the authorities. I had to show whatever I was carrying on my person, and the guard grabbed me when he saw my currency. The burden of proof was on me, and I had to find the man who arrested me originally and have him assure the guard I was taking out only the funds I had brought with me. I commented to the guard, in passing, that it was a pity there was so much tragedy in Palestine. He turned and gave me a tongue-lashing for making a judgment on the British control of the area and that it was a British situation and no business of mine or anyone else's. He was wrong since the mandate had been approved by fifty-one nations, and the British were supposed to answer to them for their stewardship of Palestine. Perhaps since the League of Nations was defunct the point was debatable, but I was not about to become involved in any pointless discussions. I was going home. When I got up the gangway I was met by a couple of strangers who told me I would have adequate escort all the way home. I was taken to my quarters which would sleep forty, and I was given the top bunk in the middle to be surrounded by thirty-nine students, all of whom were members of the Haganah and going to the United States for various reasons.

I was introduced to the commander of the group who drew me over to some people and said, "I'd like you to meet my father, Dr. Chaim Yaski," a name well known to me as well as to many people both in Palestine and abroad. He was the head of Hadassah Hospital on Mt. Scopus. His son who would be studying medicine in the States would be responsible for my safety on the trip. Dr. Yaski, the last person whose hand I shook in Palestine in July, would be dead by April and his son would have to return home soon after to take part in the 1948 War. Dr. Yaski and seventy-six doctors and nurses were killed on Mt. Scopus while traveling in a convoy, by Arab terrorists in an attack in retaliation for a Jewish Irgun attack three days earlier in Deir Yassin. The convoy was set afire and most of the victims burned to death, but Dr. Yaski, as was later determined, was shot right between the eyes. I wonder if the Arab who shot him was such a deadly marksman because of Dr. Yaski, who had been the single, most influential individual in wiping out the deadly eye disease, trachoma, found among Arabs and Jews in Palestine.

GRAUEL

The trip on the way home was a pleasant and uneventful one which was just as well because I had my fill of excitement. We just made a short stopover in Greece where I picked up a few souvenirs, which is not easy when you are shopping surrounded by thirty-nine watchdogs. When we arrived in New York City I was surprised to find myself the center of a news conference. Jesse Lurie, for many years editor of the Hadassah magazine, arrived with the rest, and during a lull in the bedlam of questions and answers, took me aside for a minute to caution me about revealing anything of importance about the Haganah operations. I was a bit miffed about this lack of faith in my common sense and judgment. All this was forgotten when we docked, and I saw my mother coming toward me, her face shining in welcome, but with tears running down her cheeks. She spent many months of worry, although I was able to send her a telegram, and I still recall the message, sent from Rome. "Have gone to visit Cousin Jacob," which to my mother, somewhat of a bible scholar, would mean I was going to the Holy Land. Then one day, before she had a chance to find out about the *Exodus* landing in Haifa, someone told her without preamble that I was all right but had been arrested. She looked at me that day at the pier, with my hair grown down to my shoulders, not the accepted fashion in those days and her first words as she started to laugh were, "You look like John the Baptist."

Several members of the Haganah were waiting for me to take us to a hotel for dinner where we discussed how much of what I knew could be released to the public in detail, which was almost everything about the *Exodus* and almost nothing about my on-shore experience at any time. The next day we went home to Worcester where I was surprised to find half a mailbag of letters, most of them vicious, anti-Semitic, disgusting trash. I threw them out. I checked with my church to see what the reaction was there, and found that they, too, were receiving the same kind of sick letters. That did not surprise me, but the mail that ran second were protest letters and sort of threw me. The Methodist newspaper had a picture of me released by the Associated Press, and I was shown with a cigarette dangling out the side of my mouth. Now Methodists do not drink, of course. Alcohol is so far out of consideration it does not even bear discussing. But tobacco—that is something else indeed. That is a taboo that must be fought constantly, and certainly no Methodist clergyman should be caught with the noxious weed. Stacks of letters came pouring in about my most notable vice. Not one letter concerned itself with the *Exodus*. Obviously the fate of forty-five hundred people never had a chance against my cigarette, which serves to illustrate just the lack of concern about Jews, ranging from total indifference to the open anti-Semitism I find throughout the Christian community. My present status with my church is that I have been considered retired as a minister for some twenty years, and I am not sure I am on the list anymore. I am still on the rolls of the local church, the one I am supposed to be buried from, but no one bothers about me anymore. From time to time an effort was made to involve me in local committees, but the entire staff of the church has changed, including the pastor, and no one remembers me.

CHAPTER 10

MAY 15, 1948—AT LAST

The first thing I did after I got home and all the excitement had tapered off was to send a telegram to the State Department expressing my outrage at the British intent to send the refugees back to Germany. I also made known my concern about four members of the *Exodus* crew, Bernard Marks, Stanley Ritzer, Cyril Weinstein, and William Millman who were being held by the British. There ensued a series of letters for about a month, illustrative of State Department gobbledygook, and what it all boiled down to was by the time we finished corresponding in governmentese, the refugees arrived in Germany and the four American crewmen had been released. I did not flatter myself nor did I expect to affect the government's thinking, but I had to try because one never knows what constitutes the proper ingredients for a bureaucratic miracle.

A meeting was called by Haganah to discuss our situation and our future course of action here in the United States. The United Nations was convened in New York at Lake Success, and there was considerable debating about Palestine. We knew a war was inevitable in the not too distant future because whatever the outcome, Palestine was ideologically fueled and wired for an explosion and whatever the U.N. decision, it would light the fuse.

112

MAY 15, 1948—AT LAST

We had well-founded hopes that there would be a Jewish State, and it would be our job to help protect it. Two organizations were immediately set up, one called "Land and Labor," which was a recruiting operation for Jewish, trained ex-servicemen who would be willing to fight in Palestine. The other was called "Materials for Palestine," later to become "Materials for Israel" and would become an arm of the "Israel Defense Ministry." We operated out of an office at 250 West 57th Street in New York City under Julius "Rusty" Jarcko. Sent from Palestine to help were two men, David Remez later to become a general in Israel's army and Shimon Perez, who would later replace Yitzhak Rabin as Prime Minister until Menachem Begin was elected to that office. Working with us were some members of the *Exodus* crew including my friend Eli Kalm.

We avoided any publicity and got as little as possible. When asked, we replied that we were collecting food and clothing for Palestine, a necessary half-truth since the major part of our collection, hardware for the expected war, had to be secured in utmost secrecy until statehood. We wound up with some very unusual donations. One zealous manufacturer anxious to help, sent us one dozen brand new packaged tuxedos all size twelve. I hate to belittle a generous impulse, but what could possibly be the demand for so esoteric an article of clothing in that unique size? From California, a dear old Christian lady who wanted to help, sent us six small date palms in tubs and a herd of goats. I will not even speculate on that gift, but we accepted them with thanks. I have no idea how they were finally disposed of, but we did not spend the money to ship them to Palestine. Some day when I have the time, I will have to figure out what kind of thinking prompted people to send us half-finished, open boxes of cereal. Possibly whatever was hanging around the pantry was donated to the cause.

When statehood was announced May 15, 1948, every Jewish

community in the world that was free to do so must have celebrated. For those Jews in Arab countries, prayers of thanksgiving surely were considerably more subdued than ours, but just as heartfelt. I happened to be in Atlanta, Georgia that night, where a meeting was called at midnight and the attendance was huge. The big temple was overflowing and even small children were allowed to attend at that hour to share the historic event. The jubilation of that celebration was only comparable to an event three years before at the end of World War II. I spoke to that elated audience and cannot remember what I said, but it must have reflected my own mixed emotions because in spite of my own joy, I feared the war to come. Whatever the case, the speech must have been a good one because I am still reminded of it by others when I go back to Atlanta. I remember listening to Edward R. Murrow and other commentators who relayed the news that night and thinking, "now we will really get to work." Until that moment I used to feel we were operating in a vacuum, a small part of the world, and no one really cared what happened there. Now we could go ahead with renewed dedication.

I was still technically employed by the American-Christian Palestine Committee, but it was through the Zionist Emergency Council that I was sent to Los Angeles to work with a fund-raising committee which included some of Hollywood's most prestigious citizens, two of its most active workers being Eddie Cantor and Sophie Tucker and including such stars as Paul Henreid, Francis Lederer, Edward G. Robinson and Hedy Lamarr. People we never thought of as being even peripherally Jewish gave us their support. We were in the midst of a meeting when Leo Gallin, head of the Los Angeles Jewish community was called to the phone. We heard him say "but we only invited Jews."

"This you'll never believe. That was Cary Grant wanting to know why he wasn't invited. When I told him we only invited

MAY 15, 1948—AT LAST

Jews he said, 'What do you think I am? I was born in Limehouse, London. I'm half Jewish.' "

Those were busy and exciting days, and I was certainly living royally. I was being housed at the Ambassador Hotel, being limousined to meetings at some of the most sumptuous homes, and being lavishly wined and dined. Danny Shacht in charge of United Jewish Appeal on the west coast was called to someone's home and found his host to be a quiet, well-dressed man accompanied by about half a dozen other men. There was little conversation. The men filed by him, left a sizeable amount of cash and left. The host was Mickey Cohen, reputed member of the so-called Mafia. Similarly, I was called to East St. Louis to appear at a Sunday morning breakfast and was told to make my speech, not ask questions, and go into the next room where there was an open suitcase on the table. One by one the guests came into the room, dropped a large bundle of money into the suitcase, and walked out. There were no introductions, no chitchat, and we did not know the source of the money nor, I was willing to bet, did the Internal Revenue Service. I think the funds raised that year were something like one hundred and forty-six million dollars and not solely from donors of great wealth. So many people gave from pitifully small pensions, social security checks, and marginal salaries as they still do today. Many were people who had emigrated from oppressive, anti-Semitic countries, and Israel was a miracle they had worked for all their lives and never really expected to see and behold, it had come.

We scoured the U.S.A. looking for anything we thought could possibly be of use to a new country, but we had priorities and uniforms were at the very bottom of the list. Even today when it comes to sartorial elegance, the Israeli army will never take any prizes. They started off with castoffs and though they now have official uniforms, other than at military parades where they are at their shining best, I do not think spit and polish is in the military lexicon. The only service that showed up looking all spruced after May 15th was the police department, and it made me nervous until I got used to it. In Palestine, when out in public, I would sit with my back to the wall as did my comrades and when we spotted the British police in their distinctive uniforms we would all disappear. At the Cafe Tiforet, which used to be on Zion Square, the arrangement with the management was that if a raid was expected, the string ensemble that entertained would play discordantly and those of us not willing to socialize with the police would take off. The trouble was the music was so off-key to begin with that unless you were constantly attuned, you did not recognize the signal. Frequently the police walked in before we realized it, and there was a strategic rush for the back door and over the rear wall. When I went back to Israel I saw some British police and asked why they were still in the country. I was told it was now the uniform of the Israeli police because so many cases of uniforms were stolen by the Haganah for underground purposes during the mandate, that it was a shame to let them go to waste. Today, even after modification they still resemble the British police.

During my fund-raising appeals I would sometimes be offered tempting merchandise for consideration. I recall going to Richmond, Indiana, having been told that a scrap dealer had picked up a lot of surplus planes and we could use the parts. I started to negotiate with the dealer when he suggested I look at the planes before we conclude our business. He took me to a lot and showed me six by three blocks. The planes had been pressed into scrap. On another occasion someone offered me a gift of four locomotive engines. I went tearing off to Rusty Jarcko to report our marvelous good luck, only to be told that Israel did not have that gauge track. I had some difficulty explaining to our donor why we could not avail ourselves of his generosity. Fortunately I am a far better fund-raiser than I am a purchasing agent.

One of our co-workers, Hank Greenspun, ran into great difficulty when he was caught smuggling arms into California for re-shipment to Israel, and lost his citizenship as a consequence. Fortunately, President Truman brought him back into the fold again. Hank popped back into the news when he incurred Senator Joe McCarthy's wrath for awhile. There followed a period of comparative quiet until Hank, who is the publisher of the *Las Vegas Sun* made headlines again when President Nixon's Watergate plumbers burgled Hank's office looking for some papers allegedly incriminating a presidential Democratic candidate in some misdeeds, according to the testimony of James McCord.

Almost to the day they left Palestine, the British conducted raids on kibbutzim and anywhere else they thought they would find weapons stored, making sure there would be as few arms as possible with which Jews could defend themselves. For example, having been tipped off to a possible cache of arms in Yagur, the British went there to search. They found and removed the guns and bullets found hidden under the Ark in the village synagogue, leaving the people unarmed and at the mercy of Arab raids. Between partition and statehood we worked like demons to send over as many supplies as we could beg or buy. The only thing we did not do was steal. We had enough problems. Everything that we brought into the U.S.A. or shipped to Palestine had to be smuggled both ways. The British would not permit us to send arms into Palestine although the Arabs managed without interference. The U.S. could not sanction our combat hardware to Palestine in view of British policy, but many officials in high places all over the country did not lean over backwards to enforce the laws that would obstruct our efforts.

On one occasion we bought surplus United States troop carrier

trucks in Chicago, to be driven to New York City for shipment.
A bunch of young Jewish college students in khaki drove them all
the way to Pittsburgh before getting caught. The trucks had
neither license plates nor registration papers, but we gambled on
the fact that no one really pays any close attention to a convoy
of army trucks and would not notice the lack of plates. An alert
Pittsburgh cop did, and a judge permitted us to continue the trip
under the circumstances since the trucks were bought and paid
for.

One of our most dedicated comrades and a constant financial
supporter was Zimel Resnick from Asbury Park, N.J., where he
owned an amusement park. Many secret conferences were held
on the merry-go-round although some have, with the passage of
time, decided it was a roller coaster. I guess that would be more
exciting, but not even my dedication to Israel would get me up
in one of those things. As we accumulated explosives, Zimel hid
them on a farm in his area with the cooperation of a Jewish
farmer, until we made arrangements to move them out of the
country. Zimel delivered the TNT himself, driving the truck
through the Holland Tunnel from New Jersey to New York
harbor, then back home to wait for another truckload. Thank God
there were no accidents because there was enough on one truck
to blow up the tunnel.

Zimel had two dreams. All his life from the time he was a
youngster in Russia he was a Zionist and dreamed of seeing a
Jewish State and touching the Wailing Wall, which he did. He
always dreamed of standing on the sacred spot where Moses
received the Ten Commandments, and he did. Mt. Jebal Musa
as the Arabs called it, was off limits to Jews, but after they lost
the war of 1956 and the mountain to Israel, Zimel Reznick was
ready. He was sixty-two years old when he made his first and only
parachute drop to the top of the Holy Mountain, after which the
monks of Santa Catarina Monastery at the foot of Mount Moses

MAY 15, 1948—AT LAST

led him down from that hallowed spot. Zimel died at seventy-seven, a man who had achieved his dreams.

When the war broke out in 1948, we had accumulated a respectable amount of arms and ammunition for Israel to fight with, but none of it reached the Middle East for a week after hostilities started. All along the route ships carrying cargo for Jews in Palestine were delayed by all sorts of problems, like loading strikes or embargos designed to slow down delivery. Our armor plating was stuck in Hawaii. When it finally arrived, the Israelis used it on trucks until the real tanks arrived. Much of our ammunition was still in New Jersey, and the rifles we were gouged ten times the price for were still in Czechoslovakia. Everything arrived eventually, but initially the Israeli forces consisted of four cannons, one tank, and anywhere from one to six Piper Cub planes, depending on whose statistics you want to believe. The war was finally won, and one of the plagues of the Middle East was born—the Palestine refugee problem.

CHAPTER 11

ARAB INTRANSIGENCE

W̲hen their Arab neighbors welcomed the new State
of Israel into their midst by declaring a Holy War, it was only the
formal declaration of ongoing hostilities that started after World
War I. The Grand Mufti of Jerusalem, Haj Amin el-Huseini,
refused to accept a Jewish Home in what he considered his turf
and opposed the British Balfour Declaration of 1917 which said
in part, "His Majesty's Government view with favor the establishment in Palestine of a national homeland for the Jewish People,
and will use their best endeavours to facilitate the achievement
of this object . . ." Obviously not all succeeding British governments gave overwhelming support to this pledge. The United
Nations Declaration of Partition on November 29, 1947 divided
Palestine in two. The Arab Palestinian State was to be the area
known in large part as the West Bank and part of the Gaza Strip
where the PLO wants an Arab State today. Instead of permitting
an independent state, Transjordan (later to be known as Jordan)
annexed the West Bank and Egypt annexed the Gaza, with
no outraged demand for the return of either forthcoming
from the hallowed halls of the United Nations. It was only when
Israel took that area after she won the war in 1967 that the
world demanded its return. Another graphic example, I believe,

of the double standard the civilized world lays down for Jews.

The second part of the partition was for a Jewish State, reduced in area to a strip in some instances only eight miles wide and virtually indefensible, with a narrow corridor giving the Jews access to Jerusalem which was to be an open city. When the Jewish Quarter of the Old City of Jerusalem fell to Jordan as a result of the 1948 war, she destroyed every synagogue and religious school in the area, desecrated every symbol of Judaism, and closed the "open" city to Jews. The outcry at this treatment on the part of the rest of the world's governments was underwhelming. The loss of Jerusalem and the subsequent loss of access to the Wailing Wall was heartbreaking to the Jewish community, but the leadership accepted the boundaries as outlined. As Dr. Chaim Weitzman paraphrased it, "Half a loaf is better than no bread at all."

Between 1917 and 1947 Jews in Palestine went about the business of living and building, intent on making the desert bloom and creating a future. They built settlements in totally arid areas left that way for centuries under Arab and Turkish rule. Then only occupied by tents, sheep, camels and donkeys, the settlements today are modern cities with no donkeys left but plenty of asses. The pioneers planted trees, irrigated the desert, fought disease, and though sometimes painfully short of food supplies, kept the dream alive. They built schools, universities, hospitals and newspapers, the most important of the civilizing amenities. The people came from all walks of life primarily fleeing first from the oppression of Russian and Polish anti-Semitism, and for those recognizing the scourge of Nazism while they could still leave, from Germany.

By the late 1930's the Arab leadership, concerned until then only about their own sheikdoms, emirates, and kingdoms, were persuaded to follow the Grand Mufti of Jerusalem in refusing to accept the prospect of the permanent presence of the Jews in

Palestine, while at the same time the Arabs were selling land to the Jews for a tidy sum. The vast masses of Moslems had little knowledge of, and little to gain from these political maneuvers. They were illiterate, subjugated, and afflicted by all the physical and social diseases of extreme poverty.

During the period of partition and statehood, from November 29, 1947 to May 15, 1948 the Arabs stepped up their attacks against Jewish settlements. Buses running from Tel Aviv to Jaffa would, for example, on approaching certain sectors, have to put up steel shutters on the windows and run the gauntlet of machine gun and rifle fire, while the British police were afflicted with paralysis until the bus passed. There were never more than three or four thousand guerillas involved in the bloody activity of that period, but they were well armed and led by the nephew of the Grand Mufti, Abdul Kadir al-Husseini, with some help from selected Syrians including Fawzi al-Qawuqji. Until they were free from British restraint the Israelis could only defend themselves as best they could. Jewish extremists were meeting their Arab counterparts head on with some excesses that would come back to haunt them. The British, still responsible for maintaining peace, intervened only when the Arabs were endangered or after Jewish settlements had been decimated as in the case of Gush Etzion.

May 16, 1948, a day after rejoicing in her new freedom, Israel was at war with Egypt, Syria, the Jordanian Arab Legion, including a contingent from Iraq, and Saudi Arabia, whose token contribution of men were under Egyptian command, and it took the first fourteen months of Israel's new life before the war ended with a thorough defeat of the Arabs. Before undertaking that full scale war, the Mufti sent word to the Arabs in Israel to leave their homes to return in a few weeks when the Israelis had been defeated and all of Palestine would be theirs. Israel asked them to remain as full citizens sharing the benefits and responsibilities with their Jewish neighbors. Many left to end up in refugee

ARAB INTRANSIGENCE

camps, some motivated by greed, others from fear of reprisals for disobeying the Mufti. In that feudal society, punishment can be swift and merciless. There were those Arabs also that would not live with Jews under any circumstances. Arabs and their spokesmen fail to mention those facts in their anti-Israel arguments, just as they refuse to acknowledge Israel's right to exist.

I contend unequivocally and believe that there is no such entity as Arab-Palestinian refugees. By definition a refugee is one who has been persecuted and had to flee for his life, or was cast out of his native land to find himself in an alien culture unable to practice his own customs and speak his own language. People such as those who were forced to integrate themselves culturally, politically, and economically in a foreign country as did the World War II displaced persons. There is no single Arab in those so-called refugee camps that is more than two hours away from his previous home. He is still in his own climate, eating his accustomed food, speaking his own language, following his own customs and culture, and freely practicing his own religion. The neighboring Arab countries comprise a total of approximately 1,368,667 square miles, Israel, post 1967 is 30,000 square miles, and in spite of her insuperable problems, from day one has opened her doors to Jews all over the world in need of a haven. In May 19, 1945 there were 870,000 Jews in the Arab countries and between May 1948 and May 1972 Israel took in 585,533 Jews who wanted to go home. The Arabs have beaten their breasts and cried copious tears over the plight of their Palestinian brothers in Islam but have yet to open their doors to them. Far better to keep them in overcrowded camps and use them as a political tool for world sympathy and an anti-Israel weapon. When a portion of a camp was destroyed by fire, instead of offering asylum to the burned out victims, the Kuwait government gave a million dollars to rebuild and keep the Palestinians in their place.

Financial support to maintain the camps and their people

comes from the United Nations Relief and Rehabilitation Administration (UNRRA) funded, of course, by contributing member nations. During the summer of 1977 I spent some time in the West Bank and Gaza to see the camps myself. I was astonished to see that many of the poor refugees have been able to build successful businesses but still go once a month to pick up flour and sugar, not out of need, but to remain on UNRRA rolls as needy refugees. It makes me wonder how accurate those lists are and if UNRRA may not have become so entrenched in that part of the world as to have become self-perpetuating after all these years.

Part of the mystique of any refugee culture, real or contrived, are the losses people are purported to have sustained. I travel around the United States coast to coast lecturing to college students and am amazed at how many Israeli orange orchards have been lost by fathers of Arab students. Granted that Arabs grow oranges, some even have groves, but if all the groves that were claimed to have been lost just around Haifa were laid end to end, they would stretch all the way to the Rock of Gibraltar. Actually, though, citron was one of the seven fruits of the Bible; the entire orange industry as it is known in Israel today, was started by Jewish settlers during the 1880's taking advantage of the climate. I remember one Arab student telling me how much his family lost in Ramallah. When I asked him when he had last seen Ramallah, he told me he had sneaked back for a visit. I assumed he had crossed into Israel at one of the bridges she keeps open so that her enemies could go back and forth during visitation periods. Close to six million crossings have been made in this manner. I asked him about a restaurant in Ramallah which is as well known as the Waldorf-Astoria in New York City and realized by his confusion he had never been in Ramallah in his life. That was the area assigned to him for his particular spot of propaganda and what a clever ploy that is. There are not too many college students that have traveled the Middle East who would recognize a lie when they hear it.

Arab students make natural purveyors of propaganda on college campuses. They are able to appeal most effectively to their peers for sympathy, and American students are quick to identify with those whom they believe to be underdogs. Unfortunately, not all students, including the Jews, are always well-informed on both sides of the issue and tend to accept any story at face value if the source is personally known. We all tend to believe those we regard as friends or colleagues. When I check out these heartrending stories the Arab students tell me, I find they have frequently come from families who have not been in Palestine for generations, let alone Israel. They are generally from Kuwait or Saudi Arabia and are among the few lucky young Arabs being schooled in America either by their oil rich countries or rich parents. Our sympathies are better spent on the millions of young Arabs who are illiterate and have no hopes of such advantages anywhere in their futures. Leaders such as Yasir Arafat all like to claim their origins as Jerusalem and rarely are their claims valid. Certainly most of Arafat's life was spent in Cairo.

Arab leaders have found it necessary to invent stories of torture and brutality against Arab prisoners in Israel. Police forces the world over have their share of inexcusable excesses of discipline perpetrated by individuals. The Arab charges of brutality are a travesty coming from the people who are guilty of such unspeakable indecencies as those performed on the Israeli soldiers captured by the Syrians on the Golan Heights. There are Arab governments that still permit mutilation of prisoners such as cutting off the hands for theft, or staging public hangings that arouse people to a fever pitch. When there is a need for keeping peace in the North, Israel dispatches the Druse soldiers of her army. They are Arab Semites, not Jewish Semites, and deal with other Arabs with more understanding and less belligerently under stress. This is done to avoid bloodshed, hardly characteristic of any army unconcerned about the value of life and keeping the peace. This I know. Israel will never give up her homeland nor is she prepared to live with a knife at her throat. The sooner the world accepts that certainty, the sooner there will be peace.

CHAPTER 12

FOOT LOOSE

For the duration of the war I remained in the United States, criscrossing the country doing what I do best, making speeches and raising money. After the war I decided I wanted to see Israel at peace and visit friends, so I sent my passport to Washington for renewal, paying an additional fee to have it processed quickly. Time passed and I did not get it back, but since I was going to Washington I would pick up my passport in person. I had been invited to attend Harry Truman's inauguration and planned to go a few days earlier to meet with my political friends from Boston. Shortly after I arrived I went to the State Department, Passport Division, to be told there was a problem and to return at 9:00 A.M. the next morning. The room I was sent to the next day had "Fraud Division" written on the door and I assumed the three gentlemen sitting at a table were generally there, because I could not think of any fraudulent manipulation on my part that would assemble them on such short notice. I sat facing them while they explained that I could not have my passport back because I had been engaged in illegal activities that "embarrassed the United States Government."

I was close enough to the table to observe the man in the middle when he opened a dossier about two inches thick and as he started to flip the pages I could recognize the British coat of arms at the top of several of them. I presume the rest were contributed by the F.B.I. Then the interrogation started. "How did I become involved in the Palestinian problem? Didn't I think it was strange for a Christian to become so involved in the Jewish problem?" The subject of the question was always referred to as "the problem." The inquiry that followed dealt with the details of my involvement with the Haganah and efforts to get answers I did not intend to supply. A few minutes were spent in this manner, then I gave them an answer they could not rebut and the hearing ended. I reminded them that the United States came into being with the help of Lafayette, a von Steuben and a Kosciusko. I was certainly not ranking myself with those giants of our history, but any judgment of at least the strength of my convictions would place me in that category. They said they would take the matter under advisement which is officialese for "don't call me, I'll call you." Meanwhile I still had no passport.

I attended many inaugural celebrations during the next few days but the one that was most enjoyable for me was held at the Statler Hilton, to which I was invited by Maurice Tobin, Secretary of Labor in President Truman's cabinet. Maurice was a lanky, genial, informal guy who in the company of friends would put his feet up on his desk, relax and talk. We were good friends from our political association in Boston and the party was attended by a small group enjoying the warmth engendered by a common nostalgia for political battles of the past, punctuated by Morton Downey's singing in the present. Sometime during the evening someone told Maurice of my passport difficulties and he invited me to come to his office two days later, when he would see what he could do to help.

Monday morning, while I was in his office, he put a call in to Frances Shipley in the State Department to ask why I was denied a passport. She repeated to him that I had a dossier from the

FOOT LOOSE

British government indicating that I had been involved in illegal activities. He replied that he was not impressed by what the British had to say and that everyone in public life had a dossier whatever the circumstances.

"May I suggest that you might remember me. I am Maurice Tobin, Secretary of Labor. I was born in Mission Hill, Roxbury, Massachusetts and one of my recollections about growing up is when I was a newsboy, collecting pennies over the cost of my papers from my Irish customers, to be turned over to groups supporting the Irish rebellion against the British. I would strongly suggest that this young man receive his passport or I shall take the matter up with the President." A brief conversation followed and half an hour later I was back at the State Department being given my passport by Mrs. Shipley and told to please report to a Mr. Robinson before leaving.

Mr. Robinson wanted me to do my country a service. During my stay in Israel, he requested that I keep my eyes and ears open and report on the number of Communists in the Israeli government. Two refugee ships, the *Pan York* and the *Pan Crescent* had come from Rumania with a total of fourteen thousand refugees for Israel all purported to be Communist agents sent to infiltrate the Middle East. He did not know that I knew all about those ships because the captain of one of them was Captain Ike of the *Exodus* and a friend. Those two ships were loaded with additional human remnants of the war on their way home to the only country that welcomed them. In any event I was prepared to do my duty no matter how ridiculous the request.

At the end of the summer when I had come home from my trip, I sat down with Zionist officials who were assocaites of mine and drew up my report for the State Department. The Communist Organization represented about two percent of the Israeli population and was split into two discordant factions. At a Communist conference held in Prague, the Israelis were conspicuously absent and the subject of much discussion because there was already disaffection between Israel and the Soviet Union. My Zionist friends and I thoroughly assessed the situation upon which they were experts, and I wrote a detailed report on Israeli Communists. It was thorough, it was accurate, and it was public knowledge the State Department could have obtained from the New York Times. The Department was grateful for my effort but I do not think they believed me, as evidenced by the fact that years later they were still insisting that Israel was a Soviet outpost. All my short career as an American spy did for me was to cause me to regard James Bond movies with a jaundiced eye.

By the time my passport problem had been resolved, Eli Kalm decided to join me on my trip. He had not seen the country either since our *Exodus* days and was eager to go back. We read in the newspapers about a passenger ship, the *M. V. Guerson,* which had been given to Turkey from UNNRA and was sailing one way from New York City to Turkey. To defray the expenses of the trip they decided to charge ridiculously low fares to visit Haifa, a stop they could make on the way home. Eli and I were both broke and grabbed the opportunity. We travelled in what could only be called a cut above steerage where we met lots of young Jews and since this was only a year after *Exodus* the kids knew who we were and spent all their time with us. The Turks observed this and decided we must be people of prominence traveling incognito for reasons of our own and moved us to first class quarters, expecting if they had any difficulty with the passengers, most of whom were Jews, we would be of help to them. I do not know by what device of reason they arrived at that conclusion but the new accommodations were happily received.

Fortunately we were in no hurry on this trip, because the ship would frequently stop for five or six hours in the middle of the ocean, during which I insisted they were just reading the next page of instructions. When we arrived in Gibraltar a stopover was planned to pick up supplies, so Eli and I decided to go ashore in the dinghy. The crew, having made this exaggerated assessment of our importance, frequently asked for our help in some manner. Before we took off they gave us a note written in phonetic English for a piece of equipment they wanted us to pick up for them. The note read "a greze cilindah" (grease cylinder) which I thought was pretty darn close.

The trip was also memorable for its menus. Turks like lamb, so for this voyage they brought along live sheep and slaughtered enough every few days to feed the hundred or so passengers. We could not complain that the meat was not fresh, but my thoughts about the sheep brains we had every day for breakfast do not bear repeating. They must also have filled the hold with watermelon. There is no other way I could account for the fact that we ate watermelon every breakfast, lunch and dinner for thirty days. When we reached Haifa the crew came to me and Eli to ask for help when the Israelis would not let them come ashore. We interceded for them and the decision was reversed, with the authorities simply impounding their passports until they were ready to sail. We vindicated their belief in our importance, which I thought was pretty nice of us in the face of all those brains for breakfast.

Once in Israel I lost Eli who went to work for the secret service, Shin Bet, which is involved in internal security. One of the responsibilities of a new country that wants to make the grade is to keep an eye on the neighbors. You and I call it spying, but governments feel it appears more impressive when listed in the budget as counter-intelligence, espionage or secret service. In those days part of the job was to rescue the newspapers thrown out in the garbage back of the embassy buildings. By comparing the empty spaces caused by clipping out items of interest with an uncut version of the paper, we could see that the ambassador of the country involved thought important enough to keep. Modern technology has done away with that by equipping every embassy worth its expense account with shredders. Eli was assigned to garbage and worked himself up.

Left to my own devices I poked around the country convinced that the new state was established and my services would no longer be needed. As a clergyman I knew from seminary acidly commented, "How long do you think you'll ride this gravy train?" I guess he wanted me to get off the lap of luxury he was sure I was revelling in. I had a very bad case of the debilitating "Thing," that Middle East disease that no one can quite describe which is worse than the blahs but not as bad as dying. I was staying at the home of Fija Branstetter who achieved fame because she used the cellar of her home to hide people from the British. Rusty Jarcko from "Materials for Israel," who had showed up from New York, got me some medicine, but they finally put me on a ship in the doctor's care and sent me home.

Having recovered my health enough by fall to decide I would live after all, I went to work for the United Jewish Appeal, but while touring the country I proposed to remain open to any occupation that seemed attractive. As always when traveling, I try to take time to see this vast and beautiful country of ours, especially places I have never been to before. During one trip to the Southwest I visited Indian country and was outraged by what I saw happening to the Navajos, Zunis and other tribes. American Indians were living at starvation level, degraded and virtually ignored. During the war, Indian sons were fighting overseas and sending their allotments home, causing their elders to stop producing the beautiful handicrafts that were so uniquely theirs. The Office of Indian Affairs had let everything go to pieces, abnegating their responsibility to prepare the Indians for the post-war era.

I thought then the treatment of American Indians was a disgrace our country would not be able to sweep under the rug forever. I am delighted now to see some effort being made to redress old abuses but I am afraid it is almost too late to do it equitably. I do not envy the mediators and the courts who will be faced with the monumental chore of making judgments based on existing treaties ignored for some one hundred and fifty years. Working with American Indians was something I felt in late 1950 would be something I would want to devote myself to in the future.

In May 1951 my mother died very suddenly while she was in church on a Sunday. A kind and fitting, though too soon, death for her and a blow to me. I had just spoken to her the Thursday before and she gave no indication of feeling ill. I had planned to scrape up enough money to take her to Israel that summer to see, along with everything else, the numerous trees Hadassah had planted there for her. She was very proud of the honor and I had great difficulty explaining to her that though the trees were registered in her name I could not promise to point out precisely each tree. Shortly after the loss of my mother, Blanche Shepherd died also. She was the wonderful woman who first helped me contact Haganah and we had been close friends since. No one told me she had cancer and her loss was an added shock. By the end of July I had had it. I guess I suffered what is known today as an identity crisis, which seems to recur every five years or so, when I must withdraw long enough to take stock of my past, where I am and where I want to be.

I went back to Worcester and quickly sold Mother's house. My brother, still single, reenlisted in the army where he had served eleven years during his first hitch, having been in Panama and Burma during the last war to return home after being wounded. His reenlistment was spent in Vienna with the Military Police. I took what little money I had from my share of the sale of the house, sold off all my possessions and took off for Europe. I spent my time headquartered in Paris and taking in expensive side tours that caught my fancy. For the first time in many years I was not responsible to or for anyone but myself and I relished my freedom.

I came back to my hotel one day in October surprised to find a message from Smitty. I used to go back from time to time during the summers to give him a hand at the caddy camps, but I never expected him to pop up in Paris. He was with his brothers Alex and Bill and they decided to stop over and see me on their way home from Scotland. They felt I was drifting too long and were determined to make me go home with them. I agreed, but first I wanted them to see a bit of Paris before they left. Alex wound up with a dim view of the place. First he wanted to know if the thing in the bathroom was supposed to be used to wash his feet. He was seventy years old and I still had to explain very gently what a bidet was because it was not commonly found in WASP bathrooms. Later Alex and I were waiting under the Eiffel Tower while Don had gone to the top sightseeing. Although it was a perfectly cloudless day a few drops of water struck us from somewhere causing Alex to suggest we move. "You know what kind of people these French are," he commented.

Smitty never married but looked after his mother who was bedridden for twenty-five years. Before the highly publicized Kennedy presence in Hyannis Port inflated real estate prices, he bought a little piece of property upon which he built a two room cottage, and lived very frugally. Whenever he got the urge to travel after his retirement, he would load up his old Gladstone bag, buy a near-wreck of a car and drive it around by day, sleep in it at night and leave it in some ditch when it died. I kept track of him over the years by the postcards he sent anywhere from Massachusetts to the Alcan Highway. During one trip out West Smitty had pulled off to the side of the road, when a young fellow stopped in front of him and asked for help because his car broke down. Smitty sensed something was wrong and would not roll down his window but looked down, to see a gun in the man's hand. "I'll help you. Get into your car," he shouted through his closed window. He did and Smitty got behind him, pushed him until they came to a small precipice, whereupon he pushed him over the edge and kept going. When I asked him what happened to the man, Smitty shrugged, "I don't know. I didn't wait to check."

CHAPTER 13

MY WHO'S WHO

Israel no longer had to fill her military needs by settling for whatever the Jewish War Veterans from South Cupcake, Brooklyn could scrounge up. That sort of equipment was crucial before 1948, but now she could afford to specify her needs and deal in the world markets, so consequently "Materials For Israel" was virtually out of business. Those of us who had been connected with procurement of small arms were approached to work in illegal areas for various revolutionary movements. People in Cyprus were interested in any arms or ammunition that may have been left over. I could have become a gun runner. Cubans wanted a few of us to undertake the same underground rescue mission we conducted to get refugees out of Europe and into Palestine, only our route would be from the Dry Tortugas off the coast of Cuba to Key West, Florida.

That I did not accept any of the offers was because at thirty-four I was getting too old to live on excitement. Not that I was anxious to join the establishment, but as I got older I got less impetuous, besides not being a soldier of fortune, requiring as I do total commitment before I can become involved in any cause. I had little chance to settle down. I was asked to undertake a fact-finding mission and December of 1951 found me on the Italian ship, *Vulcania* heading for Morocco to look into the conditions of the Jewish community there. The only thing I recall about the boat trip was that I lost the opportunity to meet Prince Umberto of Italy, because I chose instead to go sightseeing in Lisbon during a stopover. I believe I have weathered that great loss rather well.

There have always been Jews in Moslem countries because of their proximity to Palestine. In Morocco, Fez was a city with a major Jewish community and so was Marrakech which the Jews helped found in mid-eleventh century. In Islamic countries Jews are wards of the sultan or king, having a special status as the people of the book, pre-*Koran* that is, and have always been the victims of a despotism either malevolent or benevolent, according to the current regime. Since all non-Moslems were infidels in Moslem eyes and Jews and Blacks were considered unworthy of consideration, I find it remarkable that any black person could favor the Arabs over Israelis when for centuries not only did the Arabs own black slaves and treat them like cattle, but also sold them to the Colonial slave traders here at home.

Confined to ghettos except during those intervening stretches of benevolence, Jews were easy prey for raids by thieves and murderers. Some months before I arrived in Morocco about forty-five made an effort to escape from Petit Jean in a small boat with a Spanish crew. While at sea on the Mediterranean they got caught in a mistral, a vicious wind that comes sweeping down from France churning up that end of the water until it becomes as wild as the Atlantic Ocean. The Spanish crew panicked and in order not to be burdened by the expendable Jews they just battened down the hatches locking the passengers down below. The ship went down off Gibraltar. The crew made it, the passengers died.

GRAUEL

In 1912 the French took over Morocco, an occupation that lasted until 1956. From the late 1930's until the end of World War II, the Moroccans who hated the French collaborated with the Germans, with the result that the French placed Jews in areas of responsibility in Moroccan civil service. Slowly a Jewish professional and middle class built up, with young people being sent to French universities to study. Here and there over the years, due to their superior education and facility with languages, Jews were given positions of some political power, always with the knowledge that a royal whim could end the association, or the life. When I arrived in Morocco the entrenched upper class Jews were kidding themselves into thinking they were secure, while the vast majority of Jews were looking for a way to leave the country. The prominent families and leaders of the Jewish community in Casablanca especially, did not want me or any agency to come into Morocco and investigate the situation. They were suffering from the old "don't make waves syndrome" that kept too many Jews in Germany until it was too late to leave.

I traveled around the country arriving at the Atlas Mountains in a place called Ourica, where I saw Jews living in absolutely pitiful conditions having absorbed many of the customs of the Moslems around them in that backwoods area of Morocco. They wore the hand of Fatima, a Moslem object to ward off the evil eye continuing to wear it even after they arrived in Israel. They were so accustomed to poverty and primitive living conditions that it took some time for them to comprehend any drastic change. Once in Israel they had to be taught to sleep on beds and for some time they would continue to remove their blankets to the floor and sleep there. Being supplied with sufficient food also took some getting used to and after eating, their clothing would bulge from the bread they had squirreled away for the next meal. The Hebrew schools, shacks that they were, did not have windows so the doors were painted blue to keep out the devil. In Morocco there were the three T's, tinia, trachoma and tuberculosis. Tinia is a disease of the scalp which could be cured by an application of penicillin, but that being unavailable to those wretched people, both Jew and Moslem paint the children's heads with purple gentian. When anyone contracted T.B. it was considered the will of God or Allah and these hopelessly sick people, like the lepers of old, were sent to live in desolation at the edge of the cemetery in hovels, fed by charity on an occasional bowl of soup, until they died. This custom was even prevalent in the capitol, Rabat. I spent one night in the Mamounian Hotel, lavish as Shepherd's in Cairo or the King David in Jerusalem and just a few yards away I could see abject poverty. It is my understanding that today with modern care and hospitals for those in the cities, the poor still live a primitive existence in the peripheral areas.

I left Morocco by packet boat at the suggestion of William Bein of the Joint Distribution Committee office. Bill and I were good friends and had worked together in Europe bringing Jews out of Poland and I respected his judgment when he said the railroad I had planned to use would be blown up. There was a great deal of political intrigue with the French still there and the Moslems maneuvering to change their own leadership and oust the French. Bill's information had been right and the railroad tracks leading to Tunisia were blown up. I might either have been stranded in limbo or killed. In Marseille I caught a ship for Israel on the Zim Line where they always treated me as a first class passenger and gave me the best quarters. We stopped in Genoa the day of Christmas Eve and it was a strange experience for me. I walked around all afternoon looking at creches and churches. At night, American ships in the harbor turned their searchlights upon the churches on shore and the Christmas trees on the end of the ship's gangways, while loud speakers were broadcasting

Christmas carols. I was sailing on a Jewish ship for Israel and feeling low.

This was the first Christmas I would not be at home with mobs of people at the house, because my mother was gone, the house was gone, and the family was scattered. I boarded the ship, *Kedmah,* and I must confess being a little teary-eyed as we cleared the port and left the harbor and Christmas behind us. I opened the door in answer to a knock and lined up outside were all the officers who were not on duty and Capt. Chodoroff with an enormous Italian Christmas cake about three feet across. Every man had a gift, with olive branches that had all kinds of fruit hanging from them with a sort of Della Robbia effect, including wine and all the trimmings. In the hold of the ship there were still dozens of refugees coming out of Europe and I had one of the most memorable Christmases of my life, sharing the cake with all the children. The day was topped with a festive dinner and I decided it was not so bad being on a Jewish ship for Christmas.

I spent a short time in Israel reporting my findings in Morocco and came home realizing there was still a big job to be done. My past association with the Haganah had been satisfying on three levels. I knew I was performing a vital service within my area of operations and though there were lulls in activity, I was never bored and I enjoyed the people with whom I was associated. There are few occupations that would offer me so much satisfaction. I arrived back in New York City no longer in the Haganah and back at work for Israel. Between May 1948 and May 1972, over two hundred and sixty thousand Jews have come out of Morocco, not to mention Syrian Jews who had to literally flee terrible repression, and the Jews in the rest of the Moslem countries who were afraid to stay where they were for fear of terrorist reprisals for Jewish support for Israel. I could continue my support for the Holy Land by speaking throughout the U.S.A. and telling Israel's story. Israel would need all the help she could get. With all her unrelenting problems she was taking in as full citizens every one of her brothers and sisters that came to her. With all their oil billions the Moslem nations would not do as much for their people.

In 1961 King Hassan ascended to the throne of Morocco after his father's death and instituted some changes. He immediately took away one third of the physical institutions of the Jewish community, appropriating provisions and facilities from the Joint Distribution Committee and from ORT, (Organization For Rehabilitation Through Training) which were the schools that trained Jewish children in necessary skills and those Moslem youngsters who chose to come to school as well. The Moroccan people were given almost no education at all and were not motivated toward literacy in any case, since just keeping alive from day to day was enough of a hassle. The Arab nations still have a long way to go toward caring for their people though thanks to oil, they are making a start.

Taking in the hundreds of thousands of refugees meant great sacrifices on the part of the Israelis but there was never any question that it had to be done. The problems were magnified by the fact that the Jews coming from the poverty areas of the Arab countries were centuries apart from Western Jews who were sophisticated and more educated. Jews from wealthy families in cities like Casablanca, Tangier or Fez regarded themselves as more French or Spanish than Moroccan and tended to remain where they were. Jews from Yemen had absolutely nothing in common with Israelis other than their biblical forefathers and their Bible, and posed a serious problem of integration for Israel and there is still the alienation of conflicting life styles. Housing and educational facilities had to be stretched for this influx of new citizens in a country already bearing the highest tax rate in the world due to a war economy.

The Israeli leadership has to be brilliant, tough, innovative and dedicated, governing as they do a democratic people who not only have strong and informed opinions, but do not hesitate to make them known in every way including the ballot. Nevertheless, I have found those leaders I have known to be singularly human and approachable. I think I can best describe what I mean by a meeting I had with Shlomo Shamir who was head of the Israeli navy in 1949. He sent his car to bring me to his office in Haifa and I had to go past security guards and a few secretaries until I arrived at his inner office, a large circular room with windows framing a magnificent view of Haifa. He was sitting at his desk closely examining little lengths of rope. In Maine they were called "painters" and used to tie up dories but I could not imagine what relationship they had to a modern navy.

"Is this all you have to do, Shlomo?"

"I don't trust anyone else to buy rope," was his answer.

Jossi Hamburger, who had been commander of the *Exodus* was a commander in the navy during the '48 war. In 1949 I met him in New York City where he told me he had come to buy a car. "You came all the way to New York just to buy an automobile?" "Jochanan, the war is over. I'm planning to drive a taxi in Tel Aviv." I just cannot see Admiral Halsey doing that.

One of Israel's heroes, Moshe Dayan, has never been a favorite of mine, though I have not had too much personal contact with him over the years. I suspect it is because he, more than those Israelis I count as friends, epitomizes the national trait I call arrogance. I think it comes from a pugnacious attitude you acquire when you have been pushed to the wall and must protect yourself from the rest of the world. In the old days Jews were always depicted stereotypically as fleeing across the steppes of some Eastern European country, clutching their sacred Torahs to their bosoms, the smoke of the burning synagogues behind them and the Cossacks or police dogs at their heels. For me the Israelis have changed the picture drastically. I now see them standing feet apart, heads high, rifles in hand and spitting in the eye of the world. It has become a part of the fiction about Jews that gentiles love to believe, that the only Jews who ever fought back were in the Warsaw ghetto. There were many incidents of massacres across Europe where Jews gave a good account of themselves. The full story has never been told, but who cares to hear it beyond the Jewish community? To me Dayan personifies the new Jew, but in concentrated form. It is said he is difficult to deal with somewhat in the sense of "when you are so important you don't have to stir your own tea."

On the other end of the spectrum there is Abba Eban, brilliant intellectual, who I feel from the many times we have met, is not too comfortable in social situations. I do not think Israel has really employed him properly since he left the United Nations. I regard his speech made in the U.N. after the '67 war as one of the greatest speeches in history. It will be read and admired as long as people are concerned about freedom. Part of his problem with his own people is that his Hebrew is as pure as his English, besides which his reserved manner does not tend to permit them to regard him as just folks. Someone said his speeches in the U.N. had even the British scurrying for their dictionaries. If Israel ever learns to use his outstanding assets to their fullest, he will find his proper place in her history.

Those who knew Ben Gurion speak of him as being difficult to deal with and having a thorny disposition. I remember him as having a boyish gleam in his eyes and in spite of the fact that people claimed to find him intense and humorless I found a very puckish quality about him. I suspect he was as people said, difficult to deal with, but again, I never found that to be so when we met. No one will dispute that he was a great man with a total grasp of every situation and the decisive intelligence to deal with it. I think all successful heads of state in order to contend with the distinction of their positions, have to be able to withdraw to the protection of some defense mechanisms to prevent trivialities from draining their inner resources.

Men who leave their mark on national destinies must learn to live with the ever present spectre of violence. With Ben Gurion it was Arab terrorism and his country's wars. Mahatma Ghandi, the name that epitomizes passive resistance, was capable of violence when he thought it necessary. There is an implied violence in the very essence of his campaigns of civil disobedience against the British in India. Even within the professed nonviolence of the participants, there is an implied invitation of violence, to be visited upon the protesters as a result of their disobedience. I have often thought that passive resistance to violence is a subconscious invitation to martyrdom which in itself is an inverted violence. The classic example of non-violence is the "gentle Jesus meek and mild" which we used to sing about in Sunday school, and I get a little tired of that phrase. I think of the towering figure of Jesus that threw over the tables and routed the moneychangers in the courtyard of the temple and why do we choose to forget, "I come not to bring peace, but a sword?" What about Jesus who in one instance when his mother and brothers come to visit him tells them the equivalent of "look, I'm too busy don't bother me?" Not the best sentiments for a Mother's Day greeting card, but an illustration of the humanity of Jesus. It is sad that Israel, the Holy Land, must have leaders that always have to be prepared for the obscene violence of war.

An illustration of peace incarnate was Martin Buber who died at eighty-six in 1965. A short, stocky man he was a giant among the teachers and philosophers of this century, more admired outside Israel by Christian scholars and theologians. Born in Vienna he finally had to flee from Hitler and came to Palestine in 1938 where, in addition to teaching in the Hebrew University he belonged to a group that advocated a bi-national, Arab-Jewish state in Palestine. The movement got very little support among Jews, but the Arabs were totally uninterested and the idea died. The first thing I noticed about him were his eyes, which is what I always look at when I meet people, and his had a depth of intelligence that seemed to suffuse his entire face with a warm glow. He looked the way I always pictured biblical sages, with a beard and a quiet gentleness. After speaking with him at great length I came away with a feeling that he was of another world with one foot already in heaven although he was only in his sixties when we met.

A man who exudes vitality and has discovered the secret of perpetual motion is Teddy Kollek, Mayor of Jerusalem. After I met Teddy in Princeton at the Zionist conference we were to see each other over the years, involved as we both were in the Haganah. For years we never talked about what our assignments were because it was the agency's policy that its members know as little about each others' undertakings as possible. It was not until many years later that I learned that Teddy worked very closely with Ben Gurion and was involved in keeping Israel supplied with her war needs. Today, he verges slightly on being stout and in his early sixties. When I first met him thirty years ago he was slim, almost handsome, looked Teutonic and could have been listed in central casting as a U-boat commander. He is brash in a nice sort of way and is never overlooked even in the midst of a crowd. Today, Teddy Kollek is Jerusalem. They are inseparable. He knows and is known to all of its people and has a word for everyone as he walks in the city. Over the last few years I have been spending my summers in Jerusalem and know the city well, but Teddy knows every street, house, pipe, nut and bolt in the city he loves and has spent years revitalizing the old city and building the new areas. Jerusalem will be his legacy and bear the stamp of his devotion for many generations to come.

What does one say about Golda Meir that has not been said over and over again? I have no new insights into this phenomenal woman. She is said to be tough to deceive. Privately she returns the affection of those close to her, but privacy is a luxury she has had very little of throughout her life. In her biography she pays tribute to Ben Gurion saying his place in history is firmly fixed. I say that when history deals with her she will be placed even above that great man, but I admit to a very firm bias toward the lady. I remember how in the midst of the '48 war Ben Gurion ordered her to go to the United States immediately. She left so quickly that she puased only for her coat and a hastily packed bag. Upon arriving in the States she found that she only had ten dollars in cash, but she came home with fifty million dollars for Israel. It is said that Israel has the bomb. If she has I would safely bet that Golda has the percussion caps in her pocketbook.

Golda, as she is referred to by all, has never been regarded as a fashion plate and has been heard to remark that she has neither the time nor the inclination to pursue the latest fashions. I got into a very embarrassing situation at a luncheon once remarking to a woman that I could not understand where Golda got those shmates (rags) she wore, to be told by the blushing lady that her sister was responsible for the prime minister's wardrobe. One thousand women at that luncheon and I picked this particular one with whom to discuss Golda's wardrobe. I hope she has forgiven me.

I must apologize for my irreverence, but in the early days in our group we had a code name for the lady we all loved. We called her Geronimo and if you look at a picture of the Indian chief you can easily see the resemblance. For years now all of Israel has known she has been ill and often in pain, yet when most people

146

would have cried "enough" and retired, she kept going until she could finally take the rest she had earned. The summary of her life and her humanity is best expressed by her famous statement, "We can forgive the Arabs for killing our sons, but we can never forgive them for making us kill theirs."

CHAPTER 14

LECTURES AND LUNCHEONS

One of the most lucrative commercial ventures around these days is the lecture business. Colleges, religious organizations, fraternal groups, industry, adult education programs and conventions eat up speakers for their programs as fast as the bureaus can supply them. There is a broad choice of celebrities, near-celebrities and non-celebrities available on any subject the human mind can devise. It was only years after I started speaking professionally that I realized what fortunes were being made by public lecturers. People like Patrick Moynihan get as much as five thousand dollars a lecture and probably only God can afford Henry Kissinger. I remember Sen. Alben Barkley and I shared a ten day fund raising tour where he got paid fifteen hundred dollars a night for which he put in a prestigious appearance and a few words. In the lecture business people like that are referred to as fan dancers because they lure the audiences into attendance. I got fifty dollars per night, made the in-depth speech and raised the money because the Senator knew nothing about Israel.

I remember another occasion when I was booked to speak some considerable distance from New York City for one hundred dollars. Instead of sending me my contract for that evening, I received one meant for Jerry Lewis who was booked into Montreal

148

LECTURES AND LUNCHEONS

for forty-eight thousand dollars for one night for which he was bringing a floor show and paying the cast. For a while I toyed with the idea of changing careers and learning a few jokes but decided against it and I am sure Jerry Lewis never knew how his future hung in the balance. My friends tell me I should consider the religion business. Just look at Billy Graham, Rev. Moon and the host of TV religion hucksters that have grown up around us. Whether they are selling religion or themselves, the techniques are Madison Ave. and the results are lavish homes, limousines and many millions of dollars not too scrupulously accounted for.

I have never found public speaking dull and once it was even hilarious. The U.J.A. held an enormous meeting in Washington, D.C. one night and someone in public relations got the idea that it would be dramatic to release about three hundred white pigeons as a symbol of peace. All the arrangements were made when during the night before the dinner, someone realized what an unexpected surprise might befall the throng of guests should the pigeons mistake them for statues and summarily anoint them from above. Harry Goldstein, a great entrepreneur who could have been another Sol Hurok, quickly drafted a group of people, called in the U.J.A. staff and they sat up all night diapering the pigeons. There is also that marvelous woman who owns and lives under the "Thunderbolt", that enormous roller coaster in Coney Island. I would be called to speak in her home to a group of her friends and at every swoop and crashing curve of that giant contraption overhead, the house would rattle and shake. I asked Molly Moran how she could possibly stand it and she answered, "Every shake and quake says, 'money, money, money.'"

The Film and T.V. Industries Division of the U.J.A. gave a luncheon in honor of Pres. Harry Truman's eightieth birthday and I was both honored and petrified to have been asked to be the speaker for the affair. Petrified because he had the reputation for being unpredictably outspoken and rather irascible. I was

149

present at a dinner given for the president a few years before, when on his way to the men's room he found himself being applauded by people everytime he passed a table. He turned around and snarled, "A man can't even go to (censored) without being applauded." Later on during his speech he also lit into the Vatican for its inaction during certain moral vacuums in our time. Of course, as one of our greatest presidents I was ready to forgive anything he chose to say, but it did not prevent me from being very apprehensive on the day of the luncheon.

I arrived at the Waldorf feeling very jittery and two of my friends who were seated with me, Harry Hirschfield and Sophie Tucker, kept calming me down. It did not help when I was called upon to speak to look down into the audience and see Chet Huntley, Zero Mostel, Steve Lawrence and Edie Gorme and other stars of the media. I finally decided the heck with it and boomed out my address and as I made references to Sec. of State George Marshall and the President I could see him nodding his head in agreement. When I finished and sat down I got a standing ovation. When Pres. Truman was introduced he started by saying, "That young man," and I braced myself, "said things that needed saying." He turned around, walked over, reached over my shoulder and shook my hand. I was so stunned I did not even have the presence of mind to stand up as I should have. That luncheon raised additional funds for the Harry S. Truman Library.

My mother and I were great admirers of Eleanor Roosevelt and I sent her a book for Mother's Day that the First Lady had written. My mother never read it because it arrived the day before her funeral. Later I met Mrs. Roosevelt when I spoke at a dinner in her honor and made mention of the incident of the book and how much meeting her meant to me. I also told her I would appreciate having an autographed picture of her. She said that would not do and suggested instead a picture of us both at the dinner, which she would sign and send to me. That dinner was held on a Tuesday and the following Friday she left for Japan but I received a signed photograph of us by special messenger. I never saw her make a note of her promise but she kept it and I treasure the picture.

I worked with the interesting and unpredictable Buddy Hackett and for three nights in a row his opening lines were the same.

"I just got back from the West Coast and it's not true that everyone's queer out there, but they certainly run you ragged. You can't tell one from the other." After the third performance I finally said, "Buddy, I'm a clergyman and you're a great guy, but some things embarrass me."

For our next session he cleaned it up and said, "I just got back from the West Coast and it isn't true that they're all homosexuals, but they drove me crazy telling one from the other."

I remember best, however, the first time I met Buddy. I was speaking that night for the Entertainment Industry Division of the U.J.A. held at the Lido at Atlantic Beach on Long Island. The affair was aglitter with a cast of thousands any one of whom could have packed a ballroom on his or her own. I made a speech that brought a very generous ovation and Buddy Hackett was to follow me. I will never forget his opening remark. "I've followed trained seals. I've followed opera singers. But this is the first time I took second place to God." There was shocked silence for a moment but then they got his point and there was a small ripple of applause. The rabbi next to me on the dais leaned over to say, "Buddy means well." I do not know how God felt, but speaking for myself I enjoyed it. I thought it most complimentary.

All the dinners and luncheons were for purposes of fund-raising for Israel and both the people attending and those performing were most generous. Joey Adams would often perform and was a wild auctioneer. He maintained a fast line of chatter and humor while he auctioned pens with his name on them, handkerchiefs bearing the names of the stars who donated them and copies of his books which we both autographed. At one of the dinners after I had taken my jacket off while I was in the process of signing about a hundred of his books, he suddenly grabbed me by the scruff of the neck, whipped off the tattersall vest I was wearing and sold it for $150. I thought the guy who bought it might give it back because it was brand new, but no luck.

The most nerve-wracking situations are always the ones involving statesmen and one with Senator Lyndon Johnson will long be remembered by the people in charge of the function. The National United Jewish Appeal Conference was being held and the Senator was invited to speak on the cultural exchange between Russia and the United States. I do not know what this could possibly have to do with the U.J.A. or Israel, but because it was Johnson the media was present in force. Abba Eban was there to receive a check for fifty million dollars from William Rosenwald representing the U.J.A. and the meeting was planned to include a great deal of fanfare because it was the successful culmination of a pledge to Israel. While Bill Rosenwald was handing over the check some sort of electrical devices were being used to project an enormous blowup of the check on the rear wall of the room. During the interim the TV cameras were being used to test run for Johnson's speech. The combination of all this electrical equipment in duplicate being used at the same time blew the master fuses and everything in the room blacked out. The chagrin of the U.J.A. staff could only have been exceeded by the tension of the security men surrounding Johnson.

The support of the entertainment industry was important and substantial and not all the donors and performers were Jewish. Loretta Young, a gracious and beautiful woman appeared at several of our luncheons. Harry Belafonte, Ray Bolger, Pablo Casals, have also been supportive and their help cannot be overestimated in its importance in terms of public relations. For some reason people are curious about the late Bernard Baruch and his dedication to the cause rather than any financial contribution he may have made. To me he has never been an awe-inspiring legend though he has been said to have advised our presidents. I am still trying to find out what he has ever said or done that was of such tremendous importance to our country. I can only conclude that it was highly classified if it existed at all. Whatever I know about him came from his biography where he tells the story about how his mother asked him to be reasonably observant about his Judaism. As a result of his promise to do so he stayed home from his office on Yom Kippur and when the market broke and he was not there to participate in the panic selling he made a fortune. From then on he appears to have inhabited a park bench where he would burp on his birthday and find it recorded as words of wisdom in the press.

A few years ago I arrived on Long Island too early for a breakfast I was to attend. Looking for my ever-present cup of coffee I was told to see the maitre d' who happened to be from Israel. I asked for my coffee in Hebrew and he commented that he only knew one other Komer (priest) who spoke as I did and he was the one they called Jochanan on the *Exodus*. When I told him I was Jochanan he was stunned, but I continued to question him because so many people claim to have been on the *Exodus* that if it were true we would have sunk in port. As we talked he turned out to be one of that group among whom was Yacabovich, the fifteen year old killed by the British. I felt especially close to those youngsters because about thirty of them worked under me in the galley. I picked six originally to do the dishes and help to prepare the food but I wound up with thirty in shifts when the kids passed the word about all the food in the galley.

I asked what happened to Yacabovich's older brother and only surviving relative, Hitler having murdered all the rest. He told me the boy had grown up and joined the army. During the Suez War in 1956 he fought the Egyptians and captured an Egyptian flag. Coming back to his Israeli lines by jeep he drove at a terrific rate of speed exultantly waving his captured flag. The Israelis, seeing the flag, shot and killed the Israeli soldier. It was the last of the family because the young man had not yet settled down to start one of his own.

As I continued to make my way lecturing around the country I also met with ministerial groups and it may be my own self-consciousness but I always felt they looked upon me as some sort of kook. Maybe so, but I also learned they envy me as well. During the last few years, perhaps because there is so much religious turmoil, so much change, so much questioning of ritual and dogma, I believe they envy my freedom. I am free to express myself and because I believe in intellectual honesty, I am free to take issue on many levels without being concerned about offending narrow-minded church members who often deny a minister or priest a human difference of opinion on almost anything including the weather. I doubt if I could ever again accept the restraints of a parish.

I know the fundamentalists get upset with me because I refuse to accept the prophetic philosophy of their world, that the first step is Israel and the second step is the conversion of the Jews. They are very unhappy with me when I say that if I were a Jew I would never convert because every loss to the Jewish community is a tragedy in the face of Hitler's attempted genocide. I would never presume to convert a Jew to Christianity any more than I would become a Jew myself. It is easy to take on a new label but I could never really know what it means to be a Jew as long as I have the freedom to walk away as a WASP—and for many I know, I would leave out the "W." The remaining letters say it all.

LECTURES AND LUNCHEONS

I suppose if my church wanted to they could always build a fire under me and remind me that I am a Methodist minister and as long as I bear that identification what I say reflects on Methodism, but they have never tried to censor either my thoughts or my actions. Except for the fact that I function ministerially at the black church in my community and they accord me certain honors, I am to all intents and purposes out of the ministry. I am, however, a deeply religious person, immodest though that remark may seem. I have been through too much and seen too much not to believe in God and Divine Providence and within myself I have a strong relationship with Him. I cannot define the rules of faith and maybe I am a bit of a mystic but I believe my dedication to Israel is God's work and no accident that thousands of years of God's concern for his Chosen People have brought me to this point in time. I never analyze this theory too deeply because when you are tempted to play around with what you think God may have in store for you, it is too easy to wind up going 'round the bend.

It would have been much better if Jesus had been accepted by Jewish thinkers and rabbis as another rabbi or prophet in Israel. At no time did He really violate the law as such so He was without sin as far as halacha, Jewish law, is concerned. If we were to strip away all of the nonsense that has been written about Jesus in later years the whole world would have been a better place and if not for Paul that would probably have been the case. Paul had his problems and a good psychiatrist reading Paul's Epistles would find him mixed up in his thinking. Jesus was preaching the Old Testament. It was Paul that made the changes. Mohammed too wanted to be accepted as a rabbi but was rejected by the Jewish community. That is a fact of history. Islam prayed toward Jerusalem because Islam was essentially Judaistic in its approach and the very rejection of Mohammed by the Jewish leadership angered him. Just think, if the rabbis had been less political the whole world might have become Jewish. That is why I feel no dichotomy between my Christian beliefs and Judaism. Jesus preached the Old Testament. For Him there was no New Testament.

CHAPTER 15

CIVIL RIGHTS AT HOME, VIETNAM ABROAD

I remember when I was a kid I read a story about something called Christ Bread. It was about a couple on their way into an expensive restaurant and the man refused a handout to a bum. The woman protested and embarrassed her escort into giving the panhandler five dollars. The rest of the story dealt with the five dollars going from hand to hand. I have never forgotten that story and despite my age and sophistication I cannot pass by anyone in need. My mother always had an extra bed and we used to house quite an assortment. She would find someone on welfare who had lots of problems and he or she would stay until my mother could iron out his or her affairs and sometimes it took months. I never knew who I would find living with us and God only knew where she got the money and Dad got the patience. In the Methodist tradition there is always a place at the table that is known as the prophet's place and a prophet's chamber at the parsonage, so there is always room for a stranger. All my life I have done the same and of course sometimes it was the wrong person or the wrong situation or the wrong time and I regretted it, but not enough to break a family tradition.

While I lived in New York City I was continually getting involved in people's problems and always being prevailed upon to help someone. Sometimes it was with a bed and a meal and a few dollars, or going before a judge to whisper a few words across the bench. Whatever the case I could never be dispassionate about anyone's needs and would find myself overwhelmed by the troubles of others. One day I was visiting friends in Colts Neck, N.J. and fell in love with a small farm which I immediately decided to rent. It answered my desire for a change from concrete, riveting machines, exhaust fumes, raucous traffic and strident voices. I needed a measure of tranquility during which I could refuel my inner resources. I could continue my work on behalf of Israel but I would enjoy a rustic existence and mind my own business.

In 1961 I flew with Ruth Gruber to Algeria to see what was happening to the Jewish community. We found Algerians indiscriminately shooting each other down in the street without too much provocation, but for the Jews they took the time to make more elaborate arrangements like putting six schoolteachers into a schoolroom and machine gunning them thoroughly just for being Jewish. It was obvious that a rescue operation would be needed here similar to the one for the survivors of Hitler. The difference was that Israel was ready to take them all in and we did not have to face the possibility of armed combat at the end of the journey. The Algerian Jews were taken out by ship to Israel with a stopover in Marseille.

I got home exhausted and received a call from the U.J.A. asking me to go to Chicago and fill in for a speaker who was ill, Chaim Herzog, who would later become Israel's U.N. Ambassador. For the first time I refused an engagement because I was feeling sick myself. My legs were so painful and swollen, I knew I needed immediate medical attention. I ended up on my back for five weeks with a nasty case of thrombo phlebitis and I was told I needed surgery. The thrombosis was so bad, the doctor told me, that another fifteen minutes would have killed me because I had a blood clot the size of a cup on the side of my leg, that would have let go and caused an embolism. I never did have the surgery which I still need, and that was in 1961. Another serious illness put everything else in abeyance.

Way back in my parish days in Stonington I had a small rectal growth which bothered me from time to time. A dozen doctors had seen it over the years since then including during my check-up for phlebitis and I was always told it was nothing to be concerned about. Nine months after that last examination my personal physician and friend Dr. Edwin Morris of Lincroft, N.J. checked the growth again and immediately sent me for a biopsy. It was diagnosed as a basal carcinoma and I was operated on immediately by Dr. Alan Kendall of Red Bank, N.J. requiring no cobalt treatments, no chemotherapy and I was immensely relieved to have it end happily.

The next few years passed uneventfully as far as my health was concerned and aside from the need to spare my legs as much strain as possible I was back lecturing for Israel. One day while relaxing at home and drinking my inevitable cup of coffee I turned on the TV to be transfixed in my seat by the corrosive, mindless hate that poured into my living room as I watched the law of Birmingham, Alabama turn dogs and hoses on black citizens of the community. I was so enraged that I jumped up and called a friend of mine, Ted Seamans, pastor of the Methodist Church in Woodbridge, N.J., because he was also greatly concerned about the battle going on for the civil rights of the black community. My immediate thought was to go to Birmingham, not realizing that hundreds of clergymen of every denomination were having the same reaction. A far cry from the response to the agony of the Jews during the Nazi era! The result of my call to Ted was a meeting held in his church where those in attendance, not too many, agreed to go to Birmingham. I could not join them because a march from Birmingham to the state capitol, Montgomery, was in the planning and I could not undertake that even though it had been two years since my phlebitis attack. I followed the news for the next several days feeling left out, but I was encouraged to the point of euphoria at the news that there were about four thousand ministers, priests and rabbis joining Dr. Martin Luther King, Jr. on that march.

The following Sunday Ted returned from Alabama and gave his report on the march as his sermon. Half of the church members were conservative and extremely annoyed with him for going in the first place. Those of us who were anti-segregationists were gathered in the center of the church and at the end of his report I was so moved that I started to sing "We Shall Overcome," the anthem of the civil rights movement and was joined by a portion of the congregation. The old guard sat rigidly in their seats, outrage etched in every frozen muscle as they contemplated the desecration of the sacred halls of Methodism.

We continued to hold meetings at the church to decide what we could do locally to advance the cause. One night I emerged from the church where we were hosting a group of young people passing through town on a protest march from New York City to Washington, D.C., to see the members of the local police taking pictures of the cars in the parking lot. I asked what they were doing to be told that the F.B.I. in Trenton wanted all the license numbers of the people attending the meeting. The F.B.I. apparently thought we were a threat to the country. I offered to save them the film and the work and gave them the names, addresses and telephone numbers of all those present. One of these days I plan to ask for a copy of my own dossier to see if the F.B.I. tucked in a note of appreciation.

I was not a newcomer to the civil rights problems in the 1960's. Back in the 1940's when I started to work for the American-Christian Palestine Committee and was lecturing around the country I used to go to the South and was considerably annoyed at segregation. I spoke at colleges and it was obvious that even with federal grants, the white colleges were doing significantly better than the black colleges limping along behind them. Once, in Albany, Georgia, I was asked to speak at a black college and towards evening the president of the college drove me into town and offered to pick me up an hour later for my evening session. It was only then that I realized we were not sightseeing and that I was expected to eat in a white restaurant. I refused to remain and went back to eat on campus with the students. That night I went to the president's home for a meeting and before the evening ended a brick came sailing into the room through the window because, as we all presumed, I had not behaved myself properly all day having been consorting socially with "nigras."

Some time later I went to Georgia again to speak to one of the most outstanding and courageous newspaper editors in the country, Ralph McGill of the *Atlanta Constitution,* to discuss an outrageous miscarriage of justice. A black mother and her two teenaged sons had permitted their mule to wander over onto a white man's property where it promptly ate something out of bounds to invading mules. The white man came out with a shotgun and was killed during a scuffle with the boys. Mother and sons were sentenced to death. Mr. McGill and I discussed it at length and the result was that with the help of others the sentence was reduced to involuntary manslaughter. The Ingram Case, as it was called if memory serves me, made an indelible impression upon me with its graphic example of the injustice to blacks.

A part of the whole era and blurring the lines of the civil rights movement, was the Vietnam War protest. I was part of an anti-war demonstration against the war held outside the White House and found that many of the young people were so overzealous, that the language they used did nothing to enhance their image or the cause. The stream of advice to Pres. Nixon in filthy, self-indulgent language would hardly serve to win support for their point of view. The most memorable evening of my association with the civil rights movement came in the chancel of the magnificent Riverside Church in New York City where I heard Martin Luther King, Jr. make his address wherein he stated his opposition to the Vietnam War. I was enthralled by his presence not because he was a recipient of the Nobel Peace Prize, not because of his stand against violence, but because I sensed in his inspired words and the glow emanating from his face that he had been touched by a coal from the High Altar.

There exists in the Jewish tradition the Lamon Vodnicks, thirty-six beings on the face of the earth in every generation whose sainthood, whose humanity, whose sense of responsibility, prevent God from destroying the earth. In my lifetime I could argue I have seen three who could fill those divine dimensions. One would be Pope John XXIII whose love of humanity transcended his own faith and included Jewish children he saved from Nazi devastation. The second would be Martin Luther King, Jr. and the third was in the church with me that night, Rabbi Abraham Joshua Heschel, the scholar and philosopher who shared the same concerns for humanity as did the others and wore the same aura of divine guidance.

I thought of the Vietnam War as Dr. King was denouncing it, and all the machinations that brought us to that unhappy state. During the time the French were fighting in Vietnam and finally lost in Diem Bien Phou the U.S. was paying at least eighty percent of the cost. The tragedy of Vietnam received enormous impetous when a handful of politicians who had learned nothing from the catastrophe of India, Ireland or Palestine, partitioned Vietnam into North and South Vietnam. The Catholic archbishop of the new South Vietnam, concerned about his Catholic brother, now president of South Vietnam ruling the country in the midst of a Buddhist majority, suggested that a million Catholics be moved into the country from North Vietnam. The public explanation was the argument that the Catholics would be massacred by the Communists that were taking over the North. The archbishop then contacted his friend Cardinal Spellman in New York and suggested it would be good for the future of South Vietnam if there were an American presence in that area of the world. Cardinal Spellman, using a close personal friend, Richard Nixon, as an intermediary, made that suggestion to John Foster Dulles hoping perhaps that Dulles might be influenced by the fact that his son was a Jesuit priest. As a result about three hundred sixty advisers were sent into South Vietnam to begin one of the most divisive and painful chapters of American history since the Civil War.

A month after Dr. King's speech in Riverside Church, as a friend and I were watching the news on television, the program was interrupted to announce the assassination of Martin Luther King, Jr. I sat for a moment in stunned disbelief and then the tears came. My companion, a refugee from Poland who had a keen knowledge and interest in everything American, turned to me in his own agony and snarled, "Why must you carry on in this manner." The hours that followed were for me as moments of Gethsemane. Some friends anticipating my emotional response to this tragedy came over and stayed until the early morning hours while we discussed the grievous loss in terms of its impact on the black community and its struggle for equality.

Living close by was a good friend of mine, Rev. Ernest Butterworth, a pastor of a little ghetto church in my community that could have been filmed for "To Kill A Mockingbird." He was a gentle black man with a love for all people. During that dreadful night I called him and found him shattered by grief. He asked me to come the next evening to the St. Thomas A.M.E. Zion church for a memorial service for Martin Luther King, Jr. When I arrived the next day the parking lot was crowded with cars as it might be only on Easter. I entered the church, put on my robes and found myself seated with Ernest behind the altar, just the two of us. Below were the mayor of the town, his mother, a sprinkling of politicians and guests all white, and the communicants of the church. The service started with the singing of a hymn and then Ernest introduced me by saying:

"In 1941 I moved into a new community in the South and decided I would pay a courtesy call on the local clergyman. I went to the home of a white pastor whose name shall remain Rev. X. The black maid answered the door and asked me what I wanted. I introduced myself and asked to see the reverend. He looked over the top of the paper and said, 'What do you want?' I said, I came to pay you a courtesy call. He shuffled his papers and seemed to be very interested in what he was reading, and never looked up again. I shifted from one foot to the other for awhile and then quietly withdrew. I have never gone deliberately to meet any white preacher in all these years since 1941."

"A number of years back my doorbell rang. I answered it. A tall white man in a lumber jacket, with blue eyes and a smile on his face said to me, 'I have come to make a courtesy call.' That man was the Rev. John Grauel and he is to present the eulogy for our brother Martin. I present him to you tonight."

The eulogy was short. I merely quoted from the now famous "I Had A Dream" speech of August 28th of the year before when almost a quarter of a million people gathered together before the Lincoln Memorial to listen to Mehalia Jackson sing and the words of Dr. King.

One night, a few months later about nine o'clock at night I received a call from Florence Butterworth, Ernest's wife. She asked me, "Are you sitting down?" I think I responded with something about having a houseful of guests. She said, "I won't bother you then." I replied, "Please, what's the problem? Her answer was, "Ernest was drowned today while fishing in the Swimming River Reservoir."

In shock I groped for words for a few moments in that peculiar reaction to bad news and I do not recall what I said before I hung up. I refused to be accompanied by any of my guests and made my way down the roads lined with cedar trees and approached the little house. The door was open and I passed through the hall where so many of my friends were standing. They looked at me and nodded, wordless. I made my way to the bedroom where Florence was seated with the leaders of the church and broke down when I saw her. Florence, knowing I had been so ill a short time ago stepped up, kissed me on the cheek and told me to go home and look after myself.

He was buried three days later and I could see as I sat on the platform of the church, there were more people in attendance than there were for Dr. King. There was the mayor, a judge, the elders and officials of other religions, the superintendant of schools, and representatives of the police and all other institutions that make up our society, black and white alike. In the midst of all the eulogies I realized that even more than Dr. King or Pope John, or Mahatma Ghandi or Einstein or any of those inscribed in the Book of Gold, Ernest Butterworth, black preacher from Pine Brook, N.J., congregation totaling no more than one hundred, only reasonably lettered, a gentle spirit with a gentle sense of humor, a child of God and inheritor of the Kingdom of Heaven, a saint, was surely one of the thirty-six that had kept God from destroying the earth.

CHAPTER 16

COMMUNAL LIVING

The farm I lived on was a pastoral delight with grass and trees and a lovely eight room house circa 1770 or earlier, with Dutch doors and low ceilings. With my height the low ceilings offered an occasional hazard but I was more than compensated by the presence of a small bungalow, a greenhouse, a stable, carriage shed, barn and chicken yard. I also had a few animal friends in residence. There were two ducks known as the Duck and the Duckess of Windsor who lived at the back door next to a bucket of water and a broom because they were constantly decorating my doorstep. There were also a magnificent scobie duck named Admiral Nelson who followed me around the yard, and a goat named Avram that I spoke Hebrew to because, as I explained to curious neighbors, it was the only language he understood, having Israeli parents. Ishmael was a sheep weighing four hundred pounds that I rescued from a grocery where they only fed him leftover bread. I also had some guinea hens, a few dogs and some geese.

The life of a gentleman farmer was great and I involved myself in the local Historical Association enabling me to indulge my love of American history. I also augmented my accumulation of antiques from local flea markets and raised a few hackles around town by being vocal and one of the few Democrats in a solidly Republican area. My health was holding up and I was minding my own business. I was also kidding myself. I was not really content with dealing with groups of people on a superficial level. I had and still have the compulsion to act like a mother hen and spread my wings over every stray chick and ugly duckling who asks for help. Soon I rented the cottage to two couples teaching in Brookdale, a local community college, and through Jim and Dee Belcher and Bob and Kathy Jackson I wound up running a commune in conservative Colts Neck, New Jersey.

Jim came to me one day and suggested since I had so much room would I consider boarding some of the students from school. There were no dormitories and the kids were local but there were various reasons for living away from home. My generation had been brought up to live at home until married or starting a job or career. The cultural approach of the sixties and early seventies apparently mandated that the minute you were eighteen you left home even if you had no particular place to go. The result for me was that at first one or two of the local sons and daughters moved in, to be followed by young people from the school who were having problems with parents, were flirting with drugs or were just suffering from feelings of alienation that were troubling but not easily defined.

The kids were generally a part of the protest period, some wearing the prevalent uniform of pot pourri clothes and long hair, others conventionally groomed, most politically aware and concerned. They either had no heroes, the wrong heroes, or their heroes were assassinated. I realized that communes were in disrepute in many quarters conjuring up as it did visions of drugs and unbridled sex, and the old biddies in the neighborhood were titillating each other with delicious conjecture about opium dens and white slave traffic. Actually they would prefer not to believe that my guests were studying, many with Brookdale's theatre group and they were also into the music of the era, many owning guitars, and had their counterparts all over our community.

I learned there was pot smoking from time to time when I was away and when I was in England for two weeks there were a few pot parties, but I was not to find out about it until long after it happened because they knew I would not tolerate drugs. I have since learned to make peace with the fact that young people are living together before marriage and one such couple occupied one of the small apartments on the farm, fixing it up for themselves. Years later they came back to have me marry them to each other. I had no overwhelmingly serious problems with any of my young residents and I tried to give them a life style of some order and direction.

The attic of the house was fixed up and became what I referred to as a way station between Washington, D.C. and Boston because all of my kids had friends in other cities that would come unexpectedly and stay the night. I always enjoyed cooking but it was a little disconcerting to prepare for fourteen and wind up with twenty at the table. I decided at that point to organize in a kibbutz fashion and try to create a cooperative and more orderly schedule. All the kids were supposed to chip in and share expenses but from time to time some could not or just did not and I was picking up too much of the expenses myself, which I could ill afford. As one young man remarked as he came back to visit years later, "Our problem was that while we organized we never got beyond the dishes." He was right, and the irony of it was that we had a dishwasher and I still used to operate it myself when I was home.

Friday was the one night that we all tried to be together at dinner and when I was not there Jim Belcher was nominal head of the household. At dinner I followed my mother's teaching and permitted no gossip or trivialities to be discussed at the table. When, upon occasion, the discussion drifted off into inanities I had a habit of raising my fists and uttering a loud roar which would indicate my displeasure. I remember one night someone brought a friend to dinner for the first time hoping I would allow him to move in with us. Sue began to embark on a long description about a dull book on mushrooms she had picked up somewhere and I started to raise my fists. I heard Jim say at the other end of the table, "Oh, God, no!", and I let out a bellow like a bull moose in rutting season. The new kid went backwards over his chair, hit his head against the wall as his chair broke, pulled himself together and headed, terrified, for the back door. Some of the kids grabbed him explaining what had happened and assured him it did not happen too often. He moved in with us.

There was always something going on to keep me hopping. Once I heard a violent quarrel emanating from the living room and the language was abominable and out of bounds in my home. I stalked into the room, angry, to find the kids from the drama club rehearsing a play. Word had gone out that the celebrated attic was haunted. Certainly in two hundred years we must have picked up a ghost or two. One night those of us downstairs heard terrible screams from a couple of the half-dozen who were upstairs. Two kids from opposite ends of the room insisted they felt a smothering presence. As it turned out they had been drinking too much cheap wine, but at the moment of the screams one of the boys whom we referred to as our resident Nazi because he was inclined to be a bully, came rushing down from the attic in slobbering fear, throwing me over as he stampeded past me when I was coming up to see what was wrong. I could never complain that my life at home was dull.

Everyone was quick to make adverse judgments on our kibbutz

and would complain to the police from time to time when the guitars were too loud. I had one neighbor across the way, a semi-retired college professor of economics whose one ambition in life was to avoid kids, who dragged me into court because my dog barked, or he was annoyed at the guinea hens which were inclined to carry on a continuous conversation night and day. I am sure they can be irritating if you want to dwell all day on the conversation of guinea hens. In court when he listed all his grievances the judge chided him for moving into a farm area if he did not like animals, and dismissed the complaint.

Once in a while I would hear that parents were concerned that their children were living in a barn on orange crates, rather than living at home where their parents "could give them everything they could conceivably want." I decided one Easter to hold a reception for the parents and give them the opportunity to see first hand the depravity in which their children were wallowing. The house sparkled, the kids were on their best behavior and I cooked a festive feast. Whatever else they feared, the parents could see that their treasures were at least well housed and well fed. The parents expressed their surprise and their approval for the most part, and one mother sent me a beautiful plant and a note of appreciation for all I was doing for her son. Most of the young people stayed the full five years I was on the farm, others came and went as their needs dictated.

During the years I spent dealing with important people I have discovered that usually, the loftier the position the more human and approachable the individual. The biggest problem I have found in dealing with the mighty movers of industry and politics, is that they are too insulated from the public by efficient secretaries, but once past that barrier I have always been courteously treated. I meet a great many kings of commerce when we share a dais at some function and almost without exception, they have been kind enough to befriend me in some manner. Farm life and city life have one thing in common. It is almost as much as your life is worth to have an appliance of any kind properly repaired in a reasonable lapse of time. While on the farm I bought a new refrigerator which turned out to have a very unpleasant odor I could not seem to get rid of, so I called a serviceman. He arrived, I presume by camel by the length of time it took him, misapplied some detergent and it smelled worse. After the usual calls and waiting for a response I finally decided more drastic remedies were indicated. I called up a most important gentleman, Gen. Sarnoff, chairman of Radio Corporation of America and told him about my problem with my smelly refrigerator which happened to be one of his company's products. He listened, laughed, and turned me over to his son, Robert. Fifteen minutes later I received a call from one of the R.C.A. repairmen whom I had presumed moved to Cairo for all the attention my calls had been getting, and he stuttered, "You c-c-called Gen. Sarnoff!" "Yes," I replied, "I wanted my refrigerator fixed and quite frankly I went to Sarnoff because I'm used to going directly to God and he was the next best thing."

The next day I had a delegation of R.C.A. representatives with a new refrigerator, new model, with all the latest features to replace my defective one. All I had asked for was someone to light a fire under a serviceman. The new refrigerator could not go through the door and the company men departed but not before they had secured a mechanical crew of two to take off my dutch doors, install the appliance and replace the doors. While they were working I got an unexpected visitor. My neighbor, Mrs. Withers, carrying a large knife came to my front door to inform me that she was ready to cut some pumpkins from her pumpkin patch for me but that she needed some help. I invited her in for a cup of tea not wanting to leave the crew before they finished hanging the back doors. She entered the house and went into the dining room to wait for me, leaving the front door slightly ajar. Avram, my goat, always curious and alert for a handout, ambled into the dining room after her. While I was putting the tea kettle on I heard one workman say to the other, "What's goin' on around here? There's a goddamned goat in the dining room and an old lady with a long, large knife. Let's get outa here." The installation was finished in record time and they took off by the back door.

I once spoke at a dinner given for Ross Saraguso, a very fine gentleman and president of Admiral Television. When I finished speaking I sat down next to him and he offered me a job with his company. I do not know precisely what he had in mind but he said if there was no opening he would make one for me. I was enormously flattered and tucked the offer away for future reference since I was always on the edge of financial disaster and might need a job. Some years later a small Admiral transistor set I had for some time stopped working. I packed it in a box and sent it to him with a letter reminding him of his generous offer and that I would trade it in for a repaired transistor. I received a new one a short time later.

On another occasion I called Korvette's credit office in Baltimore to question a bill I had received. The clerk I spoke to was so nasty I immediately called Charlie Bassine, president of Korvette, who is a good friend of mine. Aside from the many times we have shared a dais, Charlie always seemed to be sailing on the "Shalom" whenever I was aboard as chaplain. Twenty minutes after I had told him my problem with his Baltimore office, the clerk called back to apologize. I do not like to blow the whistle on clerks, but over the last few years I have grown increasingly impatient with the rudeness one has to suffer from employees at all levels who feel their exalted positions exclude them from the need to exhibit normal courtesy to customers. Whatever the case,

COMMUNAL LIVING

I find that business relationships on the customer level are getting too complex and I also loathe computer cards. I do not guarantee that going to the top of the firm is either always workable or always successful, but I much prefer to deal with people, so in a time of need why not try the boss?

CHAPTER 17

'67 WAR AND PERSONAL BATTLES

During the latter part of May 1967 the media was full of coverage about President Nasser of Egypt, members of the Arab League, and their combined threats against Israel. The Arabs had been chafing under their defeat by Israel in 1948 and now thought they were strong enough to push her into the sea as they had been hoping and planning to do for nineteen years. Nasser was being taunted by Syria and Jordan who were suggesting that his menacing gestures toward Israel were pure bravado in view of the United Nations peace keeping force stationed at the edge of the Gaza Strip between Israel and Egypt. To shore up his image, Nasser requested the United Nations to withdraw its presence in the Gaza Strip. Two days after the request, to the shock and amazement of the world, including I suspect, Nasser, U.N. Secretary General U Thant, without consulting anyone, withdrew the troops. May 22nd, three days after the troop withdrawal, Nasser closed the Strait of Tiran blocking Israeli shipping from the Gulf of Aqaba. Had it occurred against any country other than Israel, it would have been regarded as a clear and obvious act of war.

Israel voiced strong objections to this Egyptian act of aggression and Russia immediately announced her intention of supporting the Arabs against any responding act of force from Israel. U

Thant's precipitous action in withdrawing the U.N. force and the continuing mobilization of armies on both sides made a war inevitable. Israel could not afford to wait until the Arabs would be able to marshal all their forces against her, so she responded to the blockade immediately with the enormous advantage of a preemptive surprise attack. June 5, 1967, Israel and the Arab world were at war. The meager facts as I have recounted them do not include the undeclared war as evidenced by the one hundred and thirteen raids against Israel by her Arab neighbors between 1965 and the declared war in June. The "Six Day War" as it is glibly referred to was won by Israel and is now a fact of history.

The morning of the first day of the war I was up very early, tense and confused by the reports on the radio. All through that day I kept on tops of the news. Israel was moving so quickly that the reports were coming in with confounding confusion to the listeners in a combination of fact, rumor and wishful thinking. I was also terrified to hear that Jerusalem was being bombed. I received a call from Florence Warner Chasen who was head of the speakers bureau of the New York U.J.A., to remind me to be at the Waldorf Astoria for a noon meeting of the Jewish leadership that had been planned weeks before in a response to the mounting crisis in the Middle East. I kept saying to Florence, "They're bombing Jerusalem, they're bombing Jerusalem." Florence calmed me down and urged that I attend the meeting.

I arrived at the Empire Room of the Waldorf to find in attendance just about every single person of consequence in the Jewish leadership including wealthy contributors and a number of Israelis. The meeting was called to order to discuss matters that had been planned prior to the war and by common consent the agenda was scrapped and a fund-raising drive was begun. Israel would need every ounce of financial help the Jewish community could summon and there was not the slightest doubt that with the exception of those in Arab countries, world Jewry would once again unite in an unprecedented outpouring of help.

The meeting was being chaired by Jack Weiler, a self-made man of great common sense and compassion, who had made his fortune in real estate and has been most generous through the years. He had a tendency to get a bit entangled in his oral presentations and I remember one luncheon where, upon introducing author, Herman Wouk, he went on to say that the *Caine Mutiny Court Martial* had been "incarcerated" into a movie. At this particular emergency meeting donations were being announced from the dais. Jack stood up and reported that Baron Edmund Rothschild and his wife had just given a personal check for two million six hundred thousand dollars. Everyone applauded, Jack sat down next to me and I started to giggle, more from tension than anything else, I suppose.

Jack leaned over, "What did I say wrong now, John?"

"It's nothing you said, Jack. I just got a mental picture of the Baron and his wife going over their accounts for the weekend and saying, 'Well, we'll send two million six hundred thousand dollars but let's keep sixty dollars to carry us through Saturday.'"

There were also incidents of dedication and sacrifice. One woman, an employee of the U.J.A. who would normally be there to attend to the routine business of the meeting, stopped at the bank on the way to the Waldorf and gave the drive a check for five thousand dollars that represented her life savings.

All during the meeting I had a transistor radio with me over which I heard a bulletin that I passed along to Aryeh Pincus at the microphone on the dais. He told the assemblage, "I am sorry to say that the White House had just reported that the United States will remain neutral." He added, "Israel will have to go it alone." During the next six days I crossed the country and made fifteen speeches. Representative of what was happening everywhere was the dinner meeting in New York which was originally planned as an Israeli Bond dinner for three hundred guests. The meal was never served as three thousand jammed the synagogue, spilling over into the street, in an effort to share their anguish over the war and offer their money to help their people. During those six days I saw the greatest outpouring of concern for Israel in my memory—up to the 1973 war. The six days sped by in a fever of activity and anxiety and ended with a victory in the south, the destruction of the Arab air forces and the taking of the Golan Heights.

If there is ever a justification for war, there was one for this war in 1967. The Israeli troops met in the center of the city of Jerusalem and they came to what is popularly known as the Wailing Wall, but which I choose to call the Western Wall, and a rabbi was able to sound the Ram's Horn. He was the first Jew in two thousand six hundred years, except for a few brief interludes in history, free to perform that sacred religious function at will. Though it had been, and was now an all-Jewish city in a state that had embraced Judah and Israel, a land that had stretched from Syria into Egypt in the days of King David, he was finally able to stand in that place and sound the Ram's Horn without asking the permission of the Assyrians, Babylonians, Greeks, Romans, Byzantians, Persians, Saracens, Crusaders, Mamelukes, Ottoman Turks, British, or Jordanians. He did not expect to be sewn in pigskin, or boiled in oil, or flayed alive, or drawn and quartered, or given his choice of burning or hanging, depending upon the terms of his conversion, or torn to pieces by wild animals, or even gassed and then put into a fiery furnace.

Rabbi Goren would go from the Western Wall to Bethlehem, close by the field of the Shepherds, in that area which is revered by the Moslems in terms of the prophet Elias, and he would sound the Ram's Horn at the Tomb of Rachel, the mother of Benjamin. Then he would go from Bethlehem to Hebron where he would enter the great chamber, though he would have been forbidden in other days from going beyond the seventh step, and sound the Ram's Horn at the Tombs of Abraham, Isaac and Jacob. I can still remember the thrill and the choking emotion of standing on Mt. Scopus, which had been denied to me for nineteen years, and looking down into the Holy City. It was an unbelievably moving experience.

After the war was over, The *Christian Science Monitor*, Senator Fulbright, and many other people of importance were to pour, by one device or another, a kind of vitriolic invective upon Israel. After so many years of silence on the part of the Christian leadership, they now worried that since 1967 Israel had "Judaized" the city of Jerusalem and perpetrated unknown, unlisted and therefore unproven atrocities against the Arabs, implying of course that the Arabs had treated Jerusalem with tender loving care. I was infuriated because I knew what happened during those years.

Had Israel made her way into Herod's Gate and St. Steven's gate; had she destroyed the Dome of the Rock; had she destroyed the Haramel Sharif and Al Aqsa Mosque and every Arab house so that one stone would not sit upon another; dug up the Islamic cemetery at the Golden Gate and used the tombstones for houses, walks and latrines; she would not have done any different than the Arabs did to the Jewish quarter of Jerusalem in 1948. Yet, as I toured across the United States, in Santa Barbara and in San Jose and all the way up to Seattle to the universities, Arabs were producing photographs of the Dome of the Rock with the roof destroyed, a reissue of the phony photographs of the Grand Mufti Hadj Amin el-Husseini in 1936 and in 1939. When I took issue and argued that not one thing had been touched, they replied by telling me that the Jewish quarter was not desecrated and destroyed by Arabs, but by Jews in 1967 in order to get the sympathy of the world.

I went home to rest up after that hectic war period and the next three years passed with all its attendant ups and downs concomi-

tant to living with a houseful of unpredictable young people. All
during that period I was dogged by constant financial strain. My
fees for lecturing would never have been enough if I had a family
to support and they were barely adequate for me alone. I never
had nor do I have now, any social security or pension and I have
no idea how or where my old age will be spent, but I have made
friends over the years in the top leadership of the Jewish community and if it came to a really serious situation I have every
confidence they would not let me down. The Internal Revenue
Service decided to audit me for six years once, and the agent told
me it took three agents at the cost of about ten thousand dollars
to find out that due to some minor miscalculations over the period
of the years, I owed the United States one hundred and seven
dollars. It was a loss to the government in the end, but in gathering my stuff together for the audit I found interesting papers I
had forgotten I had, so it was not a total loss to me. The only
health insurance I have is what I can afford to pay for and thank
God for Jewish doctors and dentists who have refused payment
or accepted only what Blue Cross will pay them, which in the case
of my health has been far less than their earned fees.

I remember one Christmas Eve many years ago, I passed a
pathetic beggar standing outside the church as I was going in and
he was still there when I came out. He asked for a handout and
I gave him five dollars. It was, after all, Christmas Eve and it may
have been the only money he would have and if he wanted to eat
a meal or drink it up, good luck to him. Maybe that would be the
only way he could enjoy Christmas Eve. I remember another
night in 1948 when I was pretty broke and in Denver, Colorado.
It was a cold night, but I was taking a walk before turning in at
my hotel when I saw a bum huddled on a bench. He asked me
for a quarter and we started a conversation. I found out he was
a lumberjack and he told me all about his trade. I finally gave him
five dollars because in those days you could get a room and a meal

for that amount of money. The next day I had a meeting with a group of Jewish community leaders and when it was over one of them named Charles Brown said, "Look. We know how you are always helping people, so here's something from the boys." He gave me an envelope, I thanked him and put it in my pocket. I really did not expect to find more than five or ten dollars. It was five hundred. I was astonished, but enough of a mystic to think my five dollars had come back to me a hundredfold.

Over the more recent years when I have had a financial problem I developed the theory that heaven sometimes watches out for its own. I will never forget how on December 31, 1976 I was very worried about Christmas expenses and all the bills I had coming in January. I walked into the local cigar store and bought a New Jersey Instant Lottery ticket and won seventeen hundred and seventy-six dollars. Similarly, later in 1977, I was speaking at a meeting in the Red Bank area near my home, when a gentleman, a stranger, came up to me and announced he had heard of my work in my community and sent a thousand dollars to help out. I was most astonished at his generosity and very grateful. In this day and age it is considered embarrassing and childish to leave everything in God's hands, but Someone seems to be keeping an eye on my affairs.

By the summer of 1971 I knew I had to vacate the farm because it was just too much for me to cope with financially. I auctioned off all but a few very personal things I could not bear to part with, which I stored with friends, and left for a summer in Israel. I was bone weary, broke, depressed, homeless and went to Jerusalem to restore my spirits. Once in Israel I could not seem to shake off my physical weariness and then I came down with a continual case of diarrhea which did not respond to treatment. I was sent to the Hadassah Hospital where I told them of my health record and received a thorough examination. Ten days later I was called in and told I had a recurrence of the cancer, squamous carcinoma.

'67 WAR AND PERSONAL BATTLES

There was a hospital strike in Israel which created a shortage of personnel and they were already overloaded with patients. In a matter of hours, Rabbi Herbert Friedman, Executive Vice-President of U.J.A. and David Schoenbrun, the journalist, both friends of mine who were concerned about me, put me on a plane for home. When I arrived at Kennedy Airport I was met by Bess Simon and Sy Lesser, two people that I work with in U.J.A. that I am very fond of, and they tucked me into a limousine for the trip back home to New Jersey where I stayed with friends since I had no home to return to. There were a few days of examinations and tests in Mt. Sinai Hospital in New York City and hours of walking in Central Park thinking and making decisions. I went back to Riverview Hospital in Red Bank, N.J. and placed myself in the hands of Dr. Allen Kendall, surgeon and friend. More tests at Riverview.

"Doc. Did you get a report on my biopsy?"

"Let's go to the Meditation Room, John."

"That's my line, not yours. I have carcinoma." There was no choice and I arranged to enter the hospital for surgery.

There have been times in my life when I drank too much, but I was told I was not a candidate for Alcoholics Anonymous because I would drink too much during a crisis, then stop until the next disaster in my life which could be years later. The day before I was due to go to the hospital I began to think about the surgery ahead and what it would be like to live with a colostomy for the rest of my life. My courage needed a boost and by the time I got to Riverview I was floating on brandy. In addition, never having been a good patient, the liquid booster made me thoroughly obstreperous. I was mildly uncooperative when they started to question me for the records, but when they put me in a room with three other people I was told later I was thoroughly impossible. I made such an uproar, one of the patients asked to be moved out in the hall. The nurses came to get me set up for the night and gave me a shot of something, when I suddenly changed my mind and decided to go home. I managed to put on my jacket and started for the elevator when the effect of the booze combined with the drug hit me and I buckled under, slid neatly down the side of the closed elevator door in a sort of slow motion, collapsed and that is all I remember.

After the surgery I was placed in a semi-private room and the party began. As in my previous periods of hospitalization, visitors were supposed to be confined to two at a time, but somehow I entertained crowds. The kids who used to live with me came up in bunches through whatever back door they could find. Visiting clergymen came up through normal means but apparently they were permitted to visit at any time. The nurses thought as a preacher I had a very peculiar parish. Half my visitors were black, half the kids were called hippies because they wore long hair and jeans, and they were of different religions. I was also something of a celebrity because I was told there was a call from Teddy Kollek from Jerusalem, but I could not talk to him at the time.

My roommate was in for some minor surgery and a Catholic priest came to hear his confession. Being ambulatory, I put on my robe and left, not wishing to inhibit the young man. When I returned he was bathed in perspiration and said the priest had given him a hard time. That day and into the evening there were a succession of clergymen to see me including Rabbi Jack Rosoff, and a Monsignor from St. James Church. They prayed for me and as is the custom they also included my roommate in their good offices. After everyone left for the night and things had quieted down, the young man turned to me saying, "I don't know who you are, but I feel a whole lot better than I did this morning when the priest came in to hear my confession. I feel I've got enough blessings to handle the situation."

Having been close to death three times I could not help becoming very introspective about my life. I am certain that people knowing they face death begin the "why me" questions, and having come through the crisis ask, "Why have I been allowed to live?" I give due credit to good medical care but a fair share belongs to God, and my thoughts began to revolve around the purpose for which I had been spared. The same question is faced by the survivor of a battle during which most of his company has been killed. He too surely must ask, "why me?" and if he has any depth of intelligence he will dwell upon the obligations of the rest of his life. My decision was to fill my life with other people's needs even more than I have in the past and keep on going as long as my health would permit.

While in the hospital I was plagued with the knowledge that I had no place to live, though friends were looking for a house I could rent. Fortunately they found a small place where I could go directly from the hospital. I was very weak and should have gone to a nursing home but that was out of the question financially. I spent the next few months living in a small house amid all my packing cases with one bed and one couch. One of the girls who had lived on the farm volunteered to come in daily and look after the housekeeping until I had recovered enough of my strength to cope with my own affairs. My volunteer aide was more absent than present and her good intentions faded fast until she finally took off permanently. The next three months are a period I make it a point not to remember. Friends helped sporadically, but I can still shudder at the time I literally found myself crawling down a long driveway for the mail, though I cannot recall why I found it necessary to do so.

When I could finally get around enough on my own I found a house I could rent in a far less isolated area. I was now so close to neighbors I could literally borrow a cup of sugar during a rainy day without getting wet. During the year that I was living there, some of the kids came drifting back, with the addition of black and Hispanic young people from the neighborhood. One of my immediate neighbors, an Egyptian lady who was living with some gentleman, had too much time to observe the comings and goings of my friends and was unahppy with the racial mix. That, plus the fact that I did not enjoy living in such close quarters where I was subject to prying eyes, caused me to move again. Also, the house was too small and though I would no longer be financially capable of accommodating a houseful, I wanted a few people around if only to have someone there who would notice if I failed to wake up some morning, which was thoroughly possible, given the state of my health.

Having once decided to move I gave some thought to the area. Before Ernest Butterworth died so tragically by drowning, we had a conversation about my home and he wondered aloud if I would ever consider living next door, in the black ghetto. At the time it was speculative and a sort of practice what you preach challenge, and since I had no thought of changing my residence I gave it little attention. I went to Pine Brook and asked my friends to help me find a place to live. At first they offered the parsonage because it had been vacant for a year with only a student pastor coming in week-ends, but then they found the house of a lady who had recently died and I rented that.

One Saturday afternoon, months after I had been settled in, I looked at myself, looked into the future and decided it would be just as easy to take a handful of pills and forget the whole thing. There were always pills around because doctors keep giving me pills for my many ailments, while I keep forgetting to take them. The kids who were staying with me were out, the house was deadly quiet and my bills had come home to roost. I was tired of the financial hassle, tired of my own and everyone else's problems and decided suicide was the answer. At this point, psychiatrists will argue about the sincerity of my death wish, because I immediately picked up the phone and called Sy Lesser in New York, who in turn called Irving Bernstein, the Executive Director of U.J.A.

We had a long discussion on the phone and they asked me if I could survive the weekend and come in to the office first thing Monday morning when we would solve my problems.

I sat down after the call to decide whether it really was worth going on. My health was poor because in addition to my colostomy, which I have since learned to live with expertly enough to lecture on the subject, I also still had the need for phlebitis surgery which would some day catch up with me and my blood pressure and heart were not top notch either. I not only have no family concerned about me, but the prospect of final days spent in a welfare situation such as an old age home for Methodist preachers, did not cause me to contemplate my future with throbbing joy. I also thought of my mother. She looked after the neighborhood drunk, among many others, by taking care of his wife and small children. He used to go staggering past my house daily, and my mother felt nothing but compassion for him and his struggling family. The day she lay in her coffin, I looked out the window in front of our house to see the drunk go staggering by as usual. My first reaction was, why her instead of him?

On the other hand I am a firm believer in the philosophy of the British poet, Francis Thompson, who says in *The Hound of Heaven* that you cannot duck your fate; that you have free will but you must accept your responsibilities in this life. I have the feeling that somewhere, Someone makes the big decisions and maps out your life. Some call it fate, some call it God, but there is no use in running away from what you must do. Somewhere, deep down, I must have the will to live, because when my doctor told me I had been so close to death with phlebitis, he reported with glee that my response was, "Fix this damn thing up because I have to be in Portland tonight to speak to Hadassah." When I contemplate the whole of my life to date I do not believe I would actually have done away with myself. Monday morning I went into New York and spent some time with Sy Lesser and Irving

Bernstein discussing my affairs. I received an advance and arrangements were made for a loan to pay my bills. It was a temporary relief and I am now no better off than I was then, but I have continued to go my self-appointed rounds, sometimes under the most gruelling physical conditions, but have never again thought of taking my life. Upon sober and more optimistic reflection, I have even been able to banish the spectre of old age in a Methodist home. If I cannot keep working until my last day, I would like to spend my last few years in Israel and hope to have some legs under me to get around. If all else fails I can always go to a kibbutz. I would no longer have the energy to lift stones, but I am a damn good cook and if you have ever suffered through kibbutz meals you will understand when I say I will always be able to find a job.

CHAPTER 18

PINE BROOK, NEW JERSEY

After having lived in her house for a year, my landlady sold the property and I had to move, but decided to remain in the same community and my friends found a small house for me which I have been living in now for about five years. I have decorated the place in Arab-Israeli late Grand Rapids and I have a vast accumulation of toys which I keep for visiting children, though that excuse does not hold too much water because they are complicated mechanical toys and entirely too complicated for kids. I suppose it is to make up for the toys I never had. I have an extensive library that has managed to grow all over the house like ivy. I am physically unable to pass a book store without entering "just to look," as I keep telling myself. Every inch of wall space and flat area is covered by photographs, gifts and mementos of my travels. My decorations include Christian and Jewish religious articles with the addition of icons and wall hangings I have collected. I shudder to think the day will come when I have to move again.

I decided I could no longer afford to house any more students and all my counselling would have to be on a visiting basis only, but what I did need was a housekeeper. That would mean someone who needed room and board who would babysit with my house and keep it tidy. I was traveling more and away for longer periods of time since in addition to lecturing to organizations and industry meetings, I was now on the college circuit and working in Israel for six weeks every summer, all of this under the aegis of the U.J.A. for the most part. I thought my problems were over when Kitty came to stay but I never expected her to be so eccentric. She was a young woman with a pleasant disposition but she loved animals and kept pets. Let me hasten to add that I do too, but hers were unique.

Kitty inspected the bedroom and decided to keep her pets there with her. I was not too enthusiastic about the six foot boa constrictor, but I could manage to live with the lizard and the white mice. The baby chicks running around her room were a bit much. I have yet to discover a way to housebreak baby chicks. Kitty insisted her boa must eat live food only and anyway it was cheap. The snake spent its time curled up on Kitty's bed but when no one was at home it roamed. When after a few times I pulled the venetian blinds to have the snake drop down on me suddenly from atop the window, I had to lay down the law, but Kitty and the snake were forgetful. The boa never expressed any dissatisfaction with its diet of live mice and chicks, for which I thanked God, because I had some very uneasy moments reflecting upon the alternatives.

The white mice were not much of a problem but once in awhile one would get out of the bedroom. I had visitors one day who were contemplating a very lovely kabuki doll on a small table when the doll's white beard began to move. After watching it for a few minutes not quite believing her eyes, my guest reached over and out of the beard plucked a white mouse by the tail. The lizard was not with us long enough to cause trouble. One day Kitty decided to take the lizard with her by bus to New York and tucked it into a bag for the trip. On the bus the lizard got loose and scuttled up the aisle. The passengers got hysterical and the driver stopped the bus and threw Kitty off. We never heard from the lizard or the bus company. When the boa caught a cold Kitty again headed for New York and a veterinarian. She had no problems. The snake was in a shopping bag and Kitty was not bothered by anyone while on the bus or the subway and she had no fear of being mugged. I do not know how long I would have been able to put up with the zoo, but Kitty left after some months. The sequel to the story is that Kitty went to live with a friend where the boa found its way into the oven. They turned on the oven to prepare breakfast and that was the end of the snake. I cannot see the boa opening the oven door all by itself. I wonder how Kitty's roommate liked boas?

I like living in Pine Brook and the residents have welcomed me. Just as the Jewish community accepts my sometimes outrageous ethnic stories on what would ordinarily be termed sensitive Jewish areas, so the black community permits me to share their self-deprecating, anti-black humor. I have neighbors who have been very kind to me and in turn I have had the satisfaction of being able to help them in times of crisis. My immediate neighbor Nip Phipps has an invisible, commercial garage in a residentially zoned neighborhood where the local police department hangs out. Blacks share the macho approach of the white community toward guns and one late morning they were holding target practice while I was trying to nap. I started across the yard to make a complaint when someone saw me coming and called out in a loud voice, "Here comes that honky. Let one white man in the neighborhood and the real estate values go down." My response was in an exaggerated southern drawl, "If you don't cut out the shooting I will call the po-leece and tell them the mau mau are shooting up my back yard." We all roared with laughter though no one would have said it was the most hilarious humor around, and the comradeship was easy and genuine.

As busy as I am and as much as I travel I am delighted to get home to worship when I can in the delightful St. Thomas A.M.E.

GRAUEL

Zion Church. Whenever I am home on Sunday I go there to participate in the service and on some holidays I preach there. I remember another pastor, Rev. Spruille, a very gentle man but suffering from palsy, who was pastor for a year. I would administer the communion for him because his hands shook so badly. One Easter Sunday I shared the service with him and preached the sermon. It is the custom that at the end of the Easter service any child born within the last two or three months could be baptized. Rev. Spruille whispered to me, "We have a baptism." I had a roast in the oven so with an ecclesiastical sense of compassion I whispered back, I'll read the prayer and you dunk the kid." I stood up, read the prayers and the water was sprinkled on the baby's head so fast that I am sure it was some sort of record in the history of church baptisms. I am sure it was just as efficacious as the longer versions and just as the choir broke into the last exultant hymn I headed out the back door, robes flying, sprinted up the road to the house and pulled the roast, still in fairly decent condition, out of the oven.

The Pine Brook community is a small rural one with a grocery store and church at its center. The homes are small and the poverty is large, with a few exceptions. We have the usual problems of the broken families created by the accepted welfare indecency that the father must leave home to get welfare for his wife and children, even though his unemployment may be out of his control as a casualty of the economy. I am asked, though not too frequently since we are a reasonably orderly community, to help my neighbors by interceding for them in the matters involving the law, and I am always appalled at the double standard of the proceedings, even though it no longer comes as a surprise to me. Obviously justice prefers to be blindfolded so she cannot view the injustices perpetuated in her name. I came to the aid of a young woman who had committed the crime of lying on behalf of her boyfriend, for which she was sentenced to six months for perjury.

PINE BROOK, NEW JERSEY

This, at the time that the ex-wife of Andy Williams who killed her boyfriend was sentenced for thirty days, which she was permitted to serve at her convenience. One need not be black to be outraged at such blatant inequity and I was furious. I was able to arrange for her probation instead.

I am concerned a great deal by the pattern of prejudice I find in Pine Brook. There are no particular outward manifestations in terms of violence or political agitation, but there is a miasma of intolerance hovering over the community. The level of education and interest in national affairs in this community of two hundred fifty people is so low, that they are hardly aware of the progress of the civil rights movement. It is barely visible anyway, in terms of any effect on their joblessness or poverty and so they do not involve themselves. They know nothing of the Jewish concern and commitment toward justice for blacks. The Black Muslim movement is very popular and Muhammed Ali is their idol. With no ill will toward Ali, I would be more enthusiastic about him if he used his charisma to foster a more positive approach to uplifting the image of the black community. Rather than have black youngsters dream of emulating him, he could be more constructive by inspiring his followers to respect education in setting future goals.

The blacks are anti-white and they delight in the excesses of Idi Amin and the ones who admire him most in my community are the better educated, well-established blacks who say of Amin, "this nigger's really putting the white man in his place." The most visible and number one whipping boy still remains the Jew. Pine Brook's one grocery store is owned by a Jew who has been there for many years. As is characteristic of the mom and pop type of business, Grover's cannot compete with supermarket prices and of course must extend credit. Beyond a chance reference to the "Jew store" there seems to be no animosity directed toward the owner as an individual. I know he is sensitive to the feelings of

191

the black community because when Martin Luther King died, he put his flag at half mast and draped it in black, which was something the Township government did not feel obliged to do. He also employs black help which is of course mandatory in such a situation.

What worries me is that the media, particularly television, that mesmerizing fount of education for rich and poor, black and white, does little to dispel prejudice of any kind. I get very tired of watching panels made up of black, upper-class intellectuals discuss their black brothers for a half or full hour ending on a note of smug self-satisfaction, when in truth they have failed to grapple with the basic ignorance, joblessness, hopelessness and frustrations of the black communities. They skim the surface, convene a panel for next week, massage a few more egos and go on ad infinitum.

I would hate to move out of my house, which is always a possibility when you rent rather than own one, because I would miss the ambience, the people and the humor of my life in this small corner of the Township. I was driving near my street and took a right turn on a red light some months before the law was passed that permits such a turn in New Jersey. A car came tearing up behind me, lights flashing, sirens going and pulled me over to the side of the road. I know every cop on the force but he was new to me. He stalked over to my window, asked for my license and looked at me, my turned collar and my white beard, looked at the Israeli patch on the back window, got back in his car and drove off. The next day the police sergeant whom I know well stopped by the house.

"What are you doing to my new policeman?"

"I'm not trying to do anything. I went through a red light. He pulled me over, looked at my license, looked at me, looked at my car and left."

The sergeant said, "You won't believe this. He said he wasn't going to tangle with that rabbi."

A few days later I went up to New Haven, Conn. on Saturday night to speak the next morning, Yom Kippur, in the synagogue of a friend, Rabbi Leon Mursky. That Sunday the news came that Israel had been attacked on two fronts, only six years after the '67 war. How little compassion the Arab leaders have for their own people that they pour out their national treasure in hatred, instead of elevating the miserable lives of their brothers and sisters into the twentieth century. I went to New York City immediately to try to be of some help. I worked in a "situation room" with a number of Israeli friends, including Ruth, wife of Joseph Tekoah, Israeli Ambassador to the U.N. and we managed to answer the phone calls that were coming in from all over the country.

We were interrupted by a teletype that clicked out the story that Joseph Tekoah had made a speech on the U.N. floor wherein he spoke of his country's deep regret that Israeli and Arab youth were dying. The next report that came in enraged us all. The Russian Ambassador, that emissary of peace, equality and freedom said, ". . . . I will not sit in this chamber and listen to the words of that international gangster."

I sat thinking of the old days of the early builders of Israel, when we boasted of the hospitals, homes, libraries and universities. Has Israel now reached the point where she would have to boast of her military power? That she could fill the air with planes and count those she shot down? To argue as did the commentators, that Israel had fought the greatest tank battle in history? That she turned back thousands of Egyptian troops and took a few hundred prisoners? That she lost a few hundred to the Syrians, many of them brutally killed and those returned to Israel had suffered tortures beyond public expression? That finally Israel could say she had the potential for atomic war, although Time

Magazine would report the nuclear weapons would be of low yield? That Israel could say all this made the world turn against her. That she was forced by her neighbors to turn to war made the world turn against her. The Yom Kippur war ended when the United States and Russia asked Israel to end it. Israel had recovered from the surprise attack and was winning and capable of going all the way to Cairo if need be. Had she chosen to do so it would only have been to tweak Sadat's nose as a warning, and go home again. The Arab world has yet to understand that Israel does not dream of world conquest and the World Zionist Conspiracy theory is only the figment of a diseased imagination.

CHAPTER 19

HOLOCAUST

One of the most difficult problems I have ever grappled with intellectually and emotionally was the reality of the Holocaust. Its existence outraged my every sense of God and morality. May I preface this by saying that as a child I did a great deal of reading, and with the encouragement of my mother I read lots of history including the Spanish Inquisition, the Crusades, and all the other periods of man's civilized groping for glory. I read much that was frightening and violent but I was young, it had happened hundreds of years ago and I was in the bosom of my warm family where there were no evidences of man's savagery. I was soon to face it as a teenager, however, while working with my family in the tobacco fields of Connecticut, when I saw an overseer knock down a Lithuanian worker and then beat him as his fellow countrymen stood by and watched. Later, I remonstrated with my father because he did not go to the aid of the man being brutalized. My father said he certainly did not feel it necessary if his own people had not thought to help him.

When the Holocaust first attracted the attention of the world I would not accept its truth because I still believed we were living in a Christian society that believed in the fatherhood of God and

195

the brotherhood of man. As time moved on and the whole accumulation of horror was documented I learned to accept the fact
of its existence, but I was left with a feeling of frustration because
there was nothing I could do about it. Years later I drew deep
satisfaction from the knowledge that I helped save about thirty-
eight thousand refugees from that demoniacal destruction,
through my Haganah days. I read everything I could about the
Nazi horrors, became an expert, sat on many panels and lectured
in Yad Vashem in Jerusalem, the memorial to the victims, but I
could never bring myself to go to see the concentration camps.

Finally in the summer of 1975, I was prevailed upon to take
twenty-four Jewish college students on a tour of Eastern Europe
and the camps. Dachau is a museum with photographs and exhibits, most of which I was already familiar with, such as burning
synagogues and bodies in flames. We went to cell block nine
where twenty-six hundred ministers, priests and nuns were murdered by Hitler, but there was nothing left except the bare foundation and all the barracks are gone. There are three chapels, a
Protestant one, a Jewish one that looks as if it were stuck in as
an afterthought and in the center, a German Catholic Chapel
with an enormous crucifix that I thought should have been suita-
bly captioned "The Jew Who Also Died At The Hands Of
Persecution."

As you move to your left and cross a little bridge you find
yourself on a beautiful winding path walking under spreading
trees amidst beautiful flowers, until you come to a perfect replica
of a carriage shed on a wealthy English estate and you are told
this brick building is the gas chamber. You are assured by the
guide that it was really all experimental and that no Jew really died
there. Our guide, who had previously taken us all through Nym-
phenburg Palace the day before and knew every vase down to the
last curlicue, knew the complete history of dozens of portraits and

all of Mad Ludwig's many mistresses by name and in detail, knew nothing about Dachau but had to confine her remarks to a brochure, interpolating that she was not expressing a political opinion.

Germany in June is a rose garden and I found it grotesque to go down a serpentine walk, past the gas chamber to see a garden with a small marker indicating that the site contained the bodies of those found dead or dying when the camp was opened by American soldiers. The magnificent roses were fertilized by human ashes. When the Americans entered Dachau the record shows that General Dwight Eisenhower said to the Signal Corps photographers, "Take pictures. The world will not believe this."

At that time the head of the Joint Distribution Committee, the Jewish agency that had undertaken to help the camp survivors, was Moe Leavitt. He went to Dachau as soon as it was open to begin to see to the needs of his people. He was stunned and appalled at what he found and went directly to Eisenhower to ask, "What are we going to do with those that survived this horror?" Eisenhower called in Gen. Omar Bradley and said, "Get sewing machines." Ten days later Moe returned to Gen. Eisenhower to report a lack of progress in aiding the survivors. Eisenhower sent for Gen. Bradley. "Omar, I thought I told you to get sewing machines?" Bradley replied, "There's a shortage of needles." I would like to believe the entire episode was not a sample of military intelligence, but that the enormity of the situation just paralyzed immediate comprehension and Eisenhower's puritan Protestant ethic prompted him to focus on the near nude condition of the survivors.

We journeyed from Dachau to Poland and what was left of the Warsaw Ghetto, the rubble beneath our feet. The bulk of the former ghetto area is now new apartments with a tiny park in the center of which stands the *Warsaw Ghetto Fighters Memorial.*

GRAUEL

When I was there a wreath lay at the foot placed by a group of visiting United States senators the day before. The memorial, as usual, had been built and paid for by Jews. Tucked away in the former ghetto area is a synagogue which survived by accident. One of the reasons for the defeat of Poland by Hitler's tanks was that Poland fought the Nazis with her cavalry, and given Poland's anti-Semitism she had no compunction about stabling some of her horses in the synagogue.

We entered the synagogue with some of the elders of the surviving Jewish community who are living there as guardians of the bones of their brothers and sisters. They presented me with a copy of the ninth volume of the Babylonian Talmud which bore on its back page the imprimatur of the Tsar of Russia and had been printed in 1841. On one page there is a penciled sketch of a Yeshiva bucher (Jewish student) and a carriage with an umbrella, being pulled by plumed horses, and one wonders what he was dreaming of when he sketched it. Perhaps, as in *Fiddler On The Roof*, he was dreaming of being a rich man with his own carriage and horses driving from Warsaw to Crakow the envy of all who beheld him.

We traveled from Warsaw to Crakow by bus, but I wished it could have been Warsaw to Crakow to Auschwitz by train as a reminder of the way Hitler's victims made the trip. The kids' reactions to Dachau had been comparatively minor. They were a day removed from home and Dachau could not offer the traumatic jolt offered by Auschwitz. Upon our arrival we were taken first to see a Soviet made film and what I found to be unforgettable was the footage about the twins who were used experimentally, for whatever hellish reasons the depraved doctors could devise, being led by nurses in white uniforms to die in the gas chambers. Just as the Russians have always managed to do when dealing with the Holocaust, they never mentioned Jews. We entered the camp through celebrated iron gates that bore the slogan, "Labor Means Freedom," to an area that looked like what could have been a very early university campus. There were tall trees originally planted by the Nazis to make things a little less bleak, nevertheless they could not hide the austerity of the place.

I started the tour by disputing the guide who said Jews had never died there and insisted on being shown into cell block 27 where I knew there was a Jewish exhibit. It is my understanding that sometime during 1977 the Polish government has ordered the cell block opened and refurbished in keeping with their efforts to do away with anti-Semitism in Poland. The first thing we saw were barracks still set up with berths, cots and mattresses. The next exhibit was an overwhelming collection of the most diabolical instruments of torture ever associated with over a thousand years of Christian civilization. It was mind-boggling to see what man could construct just to plumb the depths of pain. Again, it was never acknowledged that Jews had ever been in the camp, but there was a small glass case of Hebrew prayer shawls which were identified only as religious shawls and I doubt that anyone visiting the camp would have much difficulty figuring out who wore them. What clearly certified the presence of Jews was a large case stacked high with suitcases on the sides of which were painted the obviously Jewish names of former owners.

We were shown human hair that seemed to stretch for miles, and all of it white. I asked the guard the reason for the color and he explained that some of the hair would be white naturally, the rest turned white in the gas chamber from the chemical used to kill the people who wore the hair. There was braided hair, there was hair made into cloth, there was hair for stuffing mattresses. There were bricks made from the gold the ghouls had dug out of the teeth found in the dead bodies. But there were shoes, thousands upon thousands upon thousands of children's shoes that screamed the whole story of infanticide. The young people with me were very strongly affected by what they were seeing but elected to stay and see it all. I had to leave and walk the streets of the camp to collect myself. I am still being asked to serve on panels to discuss the Holocaust, and what I could do so efficiently before, I must refuse to do since my return from the camps. I will never cease to see those shoes in my minds eye. They epitomize for me all the bestiality of the Nazis as nothing else ever did and I cannot contain my composure when evoking those scenes during a lengthy discussion. For the tourist who already has everything, Auschwitz has a souvenir shop where besides books and commemorative stamps one can buy pennants to decorate the den.

The Russians hanged Rudolph Franz Hoess, the commandant of the camp, at Auschwitz without blindfolding him and the last thing he saw on earth before he went to burn in hell was his handiwork, Auschwitz itself. The hanging post is still there and the day I was there I saw fresh flowers at the base of it and the guide told me there were occasional German tourists who came to pay tribute to Hoess. Over and over during that trip my mind would revert to Jacob Branowski on Public Television in his "Ascent of Man" series. While on camera he loses his composure as he wades out into a pond, picks up two handsful of sludge, saying that they are the ashes of his family and his friend Zillard, then making the observation that Nazism is the final, the ultimate orthodoxy.

The young people were stunned but not yet through with our tour. We went to see those that still remained in the Jewish community in Rumania. They are being supported by the Joint Distribution Committee with funds raised by the United Jewish Appeal. The government magnanimously permits them to live there, but many of the Jews are old and cannot receive help because only workers are pensioned in this Communist paradise and these old people of the community are waiting for a chance to go to Israel. We went into a museum in Bucharest where a number of Jewish relics were haphazardly exhibited. Objects were spread out on tables and my kids leafed through such casual momentos as cardboards which when turned over had secured to them bars of soap rendered from the fat of dead Jewish bodies.

The tour ended with a trip to Israel so that we could end our jaunt on a more joyous note, for Israel is an affirmation of life for Jews and is in its existence an answer to the ungodly obscenity of the Holocaust. We went to the kibbutz of the Warsaw Ghetto Fighters. There they found out how the Jews fought back in one of the most heartbreaking and heroic efforts in the eternal struggle for Jewish survival against oppressors. There one can also find Miriam Novick who can tell you about the genocide of the Gypsies whom the Nazis also found undesirable and destroyed. They too are not mentioned in Dachau or in Auschwitz, but they have no Anti-Defamation League or National Association for the Advancement of Gypsy People to speak for them. Miriam can tell you more about it because Jews feel an affinity for the persecuted.

There are reported to be problems in Israel with the children and grandchildren of survivors of the concentration camps. It is said they are the unwitting recipients of the tensions created by the guilt their elders feel for surviving when so many of the people they knew and loved did not. I wonder if that is really all of it, or is it that they are suffering from Israel's wars brought home so graphically to the very young when they have had to sleep so many nights in bomb shelters and flee from possible attack? Could they not be wondering if they too are being persecuted by the forces of evil around them outside their small country? Surely they can see the parallel of a world that heartlessly permitted their people to be slaughtered forty years ago and the friendless world they live in today. It does not serve as a sense of security to the insecure to know that the United States can withdraw any support tomorrow that they have given today.

CHAPTER 20

"UNIVERSITY MISSION" AND "OPERATION JOSHUA"

Shortly after the '67 war, the United Jewish Appeal instituted the University Mission Tours, a program for college students under the leadership of Sam Abramson, a gifted scholar and an authority on European Jewish Communities. The tours consist of Jewish historical sites in Europe and finish with a stay in Israel. The students who took advantage of these pilgrimages were from families wealthy enough to afford this expensive effort to either inculcate or reinforce their children's Jewish religious and cultural heritages. The trips ran during the summer and Christmas vacation periods. During the Israeli part of the junket we would go from Safad in the north to Sharm el Sheikh in the southernmost tip of the Sinai with a continuous seminar between stops. We rode in air-conditioned buses and discussions included what we had seen, what we would be seeing, problems of Jews and Arabs, history, and anything else that a bus load of inquiring college students could come up with.

Our range of topics even included the flora and fauna of the Holy Land which is most fascinating, and I once offered a ten dollar reward for anyone who spotted an ibex, because in thirty years of traveling back and forth I had never seen one. Everyone got caught up in the hunt and we went exactly one hundred yards when the bus ground to a halt and the Israeli bus driver smugly pointed to the top of a hill. There was a great big old ibex surrounded by his entire family. The bus driver refused the reward with a big grin. There are additional joys like skin diving among the sharks at Sharm el Sheikh. The water is about eighty-two degrees, and the sharks are inclined to benevolence if not activated by blood and go their own way. The entire tour, both atmosphere and activities were designed to give the participants a feeling for an Israel both thousands of years old and as new as tomorrow's continuing history.

Problems can arise when the group may consist of thirty eight girls and six boys as they sometimes have. Delightful for the boys but causing frequent bouts of intrigue and temperament on the part of the girls. However, no problem is as insoluble as trying to satisfy forty-four appetites. If they were dining in Maxim's in Paris they would have forty opinions of the food, all of them bad. I am convinced the only solution would be to have forty-four mothers along to do the cooking. We never lacked excitement. Once, on the bus, a girl let out such a blood-curdling howl I thought we were being attacked. She discovered she had forgotten her hair dryer. She was somewhat consoled by the information that we were spending the next two days at a Bedouin village that had no electricity. Along the way we made one stop at a tank installation to see Israelis standing guard in case of another war. The weather was hot and hundreds of soldiers watched as young American girls dressed in as little as respectably possible, exited from the bus. Before I had time to wonder if there would be any problems, a young man charged forward and in a fury of Brooklynese demanded to know one good reason why tourists were being brought to a secret installation. I asked him to lean over so I could whisper to him, "These young people have parents who in the aggregate give many millions of dollars to the U.J.A."

"MISSION" AND "OPERATION"

Whereupon the answer came, "That's a reason," and he walked away.

Working with these young people from educated and affluent parents dedicated to their Jewish culture came as a revelation to me. Judaically speaking, they were the most ignorant youngsters I had ever met, though I hasten to add, their ignorance in no way exceeded that of their Christian peers at home as to their own cultural backgrounds. As for the Jewish students I went to the concentration camps with, when we were standing in the Warsaw cemetery where Dubnow and Peretz were buried, they had heard of neither. When I explained that Simon Dubnow was a renowned Jewish historian shot by the Nazis in 1941, and Peretz, who died in 1915 was one of the greatest of the Yiddish authors, the kids did not even indicate a passing familiarity with the names. Later on, when we went to the Jewish Center I noticed a picture of Shalom Aleichem and commented on the strange, almost Arabic characters with which the name was inscribed under the portrait. I was absolutely dumbfounded when no one knew who he was, when all of them had seen *Fiddler On The Roof*.

I was to find the same depth of ignorance from the young people on many of the subsequent tours, and it was a source of pleasure to me to turn them on to their own history and faith. They had come from the States armed with the frothiest of escapist reading matter, if they read at all, and switched during the trip and on the way back home to books I had introduced them to in Israel, to understand their own ancient origins. I was also astounded on one of the trips to meet two young men in their very early twenties who had never been bar mitzvah. I thought it was exceedingly rare for anyone brought up in a Jewish home these days not to have had the traditional rite of manhood by the time he was thirteen, and feeling as I did that it was tantamount

205

to an unbaptised Christian, I proceeded to rectify the matter. I do not know if I talked them into wanting it or if they were merely obliging me, but I arranged a bar mitzvah for them at the Wall in Jerusalem. The arrangements were a little difficult because I had to explain to a minyan of ten traditionalists that the candidates knew no Hebrew and needed to have their portions of the Torah read by proxy. All went well, and however the young men may have felt, I felt better.

The late sixties and the early seventies was a time of wanderlust for the thousands of young people of the backpack Europe on five dollars a day era, who were out to see the world. I can remember the Madrid railroad station where over a period of time I saw hundreds of youngsters from Germany, America, Japan, England and heaven knows how many other countries, just sitting around waiting for the next train to anywhere so they could use their Eurail passes to cover the continent. There were an equal number of young people hanging around in Israel as well. They would congregate in Jerusalem at the Herod's Gate where there was a coffee house owned by Uncle Moustache who weighed about four hundred pounds. He had a big, black moustache and three sons who were his carbon copies and a deep whiff of the pungent air around the establishment would lead you to believe that Uncle's moustache was not the main attraction. There were other areas where one would find the backpackers, such as the Danish Tea Room or in the Pizza Palace of the New City, which refers to the part of Jerusalem that surrounds the gated, walled, ancient, biblical inner city.

The University Mission students saw these young wanderers as their counterparts, either less affluent or preferring to travel as they did, and came up with a new type of tour with the inspiration of Sam Abramson and the full support of Rabbi Herbert Friedman, the Executive Vice-President of the U.J.A. They set up an inexpensive series of one day tours subsidized by the U.J.A. that grew so popular that funds were later raised for them by American Jewish students on college campuses across the country to help defray the cost. The trips started in 1970 to show the young travelers that there was more to Israel than what could be seen from the vantage point of lounging aimlessly at a popular gathering spot. The tours were named "Operation Joshua" and the motto was "Seek Out The Land" taken from Joshua's words to Caleb and the others who were going into the new land of Canaan. Over the past seven years Joshua students have come from all over Europe, Australia and Japan as well as the U.S.A. About one third of each group was non-Jewish and language was no barrier because most spoke English and those who did not were bound to find someone on the bus who could translate.

I became associated with "Operation Joshua" accidentally. I was invited to speak to a Jewish youth group at Queens College in New York and a young man, Mitch Goldberg decided I was just the ingredient Operation Joshua was missing. I was only mildly interested when Mitch told me about it, but he was very determined and in the summer of 1971 I joined the tours. We ran as many as sixty trips in five weeks traveling four days a week and one had the option to tour all week or only the trip that was of special interest. During one summer we accommodated as many as fifteen hundred to two thousand students. The scheduling would change but our purpose was to go from Safad to Beersheba. Safad is the location of that intense, mystical period of Judaism in the 16th century that evolved into the Cabbalistic movement, and was the home of one of its greatest exponents, Rabbi Yitzhak Luria. It was also the seat of many great rabbinic scholars of that century, including Rabbi Joseph Caro who codified Jewish law and Rabbi Moses Cordovero, a cabalistic theologian. Safad was also the location of the burial of several dozen of the youngsters murdered in an Arab terrorist attack on a school in Ma'alot.

We would go to the Church of the Beatitudes in Galilee as an example of modern Christian influence in the land. The church is a magnificent structure that looks like a wedding cake and was paid for by Benito Mussolini in 1936. On to Capernaum where far below the present excavation lies the ancient synagogue where Jesus used to preach, then we would continue to Magdala where Mary Magdalene lived. Next, to Tiberias where the ancient Turkish wall still stands, to see Herod's Hot Springs, all the while tracing the Jewish history of that period. Nearby is the traditional tomb of Maimonides, the twelfth century rabbi, physician and philosopher who codified the whole of the *Talmud* and authored the immortal *Guide Of The Perplexed.*

We would travel down the West Bank along the Jordanian border to the Allenby Bridge where they could see the open door policy between the Arab world and Israel as people are allowed to go back and forth after a reasonable security check. An exciting stop is Jericho, location of the digs of archeologist Kathleen Kenyon, that take us back to the oldest city in the world and its fortification of 15,000 years ago. Of course no Israeli tour can be without a visit to the Qumran Caves where the Dead Sea Scrolls were found, then, almost next door to a Nachal, a modern military-agricultural settlement, where farmers worked the soil by day and became armed soldiers defending their homes by night. After becoming fully established these nahalim are converted into civilian communities.

Beersheba is a modern city today but when I first visited there thirty years ago it looked like a left over Hollywood set from "High Noon." It was like an early American frontier town with a cantina run by someone named Ketzel who also had a branch in Tel Aviv. You could have a few drinks there and except for the fact that instead of Indians there were Bedouins wandering up and down the streets, you would almost expect to see Gary Cooper strolling down yonder, or thataway or whatever. We

"MISSION" AND "OPERATION"

would go to a Bedouin camp and sit and talk about the six tribes involving thirty thousand people who up until several years ago were quick frozen in time and whose total social structure is slowly, painfully, unraveling and giving way to a modern world of radically changing values. Next, Ashdod where, in the Old Testament, Samson ripped off the Gates of Gaza. Today, Ashdod is a city encompassing a remarkable engineering feat. On a sandy beach where no port was possible, catrapods of concrete were built out to the sea creating one of the most important ports on the Mediterannean.

The young people would be taken to meet new Russian immigrants, see how they live and study, and find out first hand how one lives under the Russian Bear that crushes your freedom. The roadways of the tours were dotted by visible reminders of the Mideast wars bringing the whole problem graphically to light. We would end at Yad Vashem, the Holocaust memorial, where I would lecture about what happens when Man runs amok. Four dollars a day with meals, an air-conditioned bus and the hope that these young people would go home with a realistic approach to that part of the world. Although we guided the tours, we did not censor them.

These treks into antiquity were always guarded against the ever possible modern threat of terrorism. One year there was a bomb or grenade lobbed under a busload of Christian pilgrims and a teenage girl had her leg blown off. On our buses there are forty-two tourists, and three armed officials, the driver, the security man and me representing the program itself. The closest we were to a bad scare was in Beersheba when an explosion under a tire split the side of the bus. No one was hurt. Our security man went outside to look at the tire and the area around the fender and found it all peppered with bits of twisted metal. We still do not go into dangerous areas and in the last few summers we have not gone into Ramalla or Nablus because Arab demonstrations are frequently held there and we might accidentally arrive in the midst of one and unwittingly our kids could be endangered.

While working in Joshua during the summer of 1974 my staff members spoke to me about a youngster named Saliba working for the hotel in which we were housed. They told me he was very bright, hard working and ambitious and they wanted me to speak to him. His job consisted of everything that came along from carrying luggage to repairs to cleaning up. I met him and found out that he was a Christian whose father was a white Russian refugee who came to Palestine as a child and his mother was a Greek whose family had been in Jerusalem for generations. Saliba was saving his money to study hotel management in Switzerland. In spite of the fact that he was very bright, spoke Arabic, Hebrew, French and English fluently, I thought given the Israeli economy and four brothers and three sisters, his chances for success lay in the realm of wishful thinking. I asked him if he would like to go to the United States and that was the last I saw of him for about three weeks. When we met again I talked with him at length and impulsively asked him if he wanted to go home with me. It took me six weeks to arrange for his papers.

I had originally intended to send him to Cornell but it was too expensive and he went to a local community college instead where in spite of being two months late he completed the rest of that year and the next with high honors. His third year was at Monmouth College in New Jersey where he did so well, he earned a full scholarship for his fourth year. He has been rewarded by the respect of his professors who had a party for him which they called "An Evening With Saliba." He and I think his future lies in the field of political science and diplomacy and who knows, he may even become the second Secretary of State with an accent. In this phenomenal country all things are possible. As for me, he has come into my life when I cannot be totally alone given the state of my health, and he has more than repaid my interest in his future by the concern he has shown for my welfare, the care of my household when I am away and the affection he has earned from my friends. He has a talent for reaching out and communicating with people.

Saliba and I watch the news from Israel with intense interest, especially from Jerusalem where his family lives. From time to time, we would watch television covering what they term an Arab demonstration against the Jews and show ". . . Israeli police oppressing Arab children." We were appalled. Anyone as thoroughly familiar with that part of the world as we would recognize them as Arab members of the Israeli police force. One demonstration in the vicinity of the Mosque of Omar consisted of Arab children, teenagers or younger, throwing rocks at Arab policemen and being given exposure in the western press as a political "riot".

When there are demonstrations against the Israelis by Arabs, they are generally against higher taxes by people who twenty years ago had no income to tax. These are labor tactics used in all western countries. Israel will know she has achieved genuine equality among nations when her strikes are recognized as a tool of protest used by a free people, rather than an act of insurrection against a brutal government; when rioting by young people is interpreted as it is, an anti-establishment expression against unemployment, rather than revolution. God knows there are enough legitimate problems and need for reform in Israel without inventing any.

Saliba's presence reminds me so vividly of the many young people across the face of this earth that should be plucked as the brands from burning. I often walk through the streets in cities far removed from the American scene and see children for whom the future is bleak or there is no future at all. Here at home it is tragic that so many young people fail to seize upon the opportunity to find solutions to their problems because they imagine it is useless to try. Four years ago I took an overnight steamer from Liverpool to Belfast and arrived very early in the morning. It was winter in Ireland and the sun only manages to rise by ten in the morning. I stood motionless in the half-light. Before me was Palestine in 1947. I saw rows of barbed wire which in Israel we had called Bevingrads after England's foreign secretary, big barrels of cement, troops standing around wearing the familiar red berets and carrying sten guns. Belfast of 1973, Palestine of 1947. I walked through the streets and saw the children, streetwise urchins who had never known peace. My God! What of their futures!

CHAPTER 21

ANTI-SEMITISM

Ninety-nine percent of the Protestant community and probably ninety percent of the Catholic community are anti-Semitic to some degree. I base this not on statistics but on my own very broad experiences of thirty years of travel across the country while being attuned to the nuances of all kinds of racism. Of our thirty-nine presidents all but one have been white Anglo-Saxon Protestants. The lone Catholic made it by a fluke created by the personal charisma of John Kennedy and the mood of the country after eight somnambulant years with "father" Eisenhower. The country was calling for youth, excitement and a change of pace. The degree of anti-Semitism may vary from finite and deeply buried in the individual consciousness to rampantly virulent, but it exists.

Some of my best friends are gentiles and feel free to express themselves to me in terms of tasteless jokes or blatant stereotypical remarks about Jews being thus and so. I can remember an incident as far back as my association with Boston politics after I had already been working with the Jewish community. I was in a hotel room with Paul Dever, a future governor of Massachusetts, William "Onion" Burke, State Democratic Chairman, and Jeff Sullivan, Mayor of Worcester. Burke said, "You're lucky to get in with the Jews, because when "they" start cracking down on them, they're going to need someone to front for their businesses." At first I took it for a nasty effort at humor, although Dever and Sullivan were not laughing. Anti-Semitism has been nurtured by the churches. Two of the greatest anti-Semites in history as judged by their own statements were St. John Crysostom and Martin Luther and over the years this has become established policy of the church.

When Dr. Theodor Herzl, founder of present day Zionism, went to see Pope Leo XIII, the Pope let him know he would have nothing to do with Jews. WASPS do have one mitigating factor in their anti-Semitism. They equally resent every cultural approach other than their own. I am frequently assured by Christian friends that they are not in the least anti-Semitic and harbor only the greatest admiration for their "Jew" doctors and their "Jew" accountants. They would be genuinely astonished were I to ask after the health of the "Christian" wives and their "Christian" children.

For years I was the chaplain on Israel's Zim Line ships. I would advise them when I had the urge to travel and in return for free passage I would take care of the Christians on board and deliver a lecture to all of the passengers as part of the ship's social activities program. The *Shalom,* the queen of the line, had an especially beautiful chapel, although most passengers did not know it existed. The walls, floor and ceiling were carpeted in gold, there were soft hidden lights and an altar which could be changed from a plain cross to a crucifix depending upon the need of the passengers. The chapel had been dedicated by Cardinal Tisserant, a very important member of the Vatican hierarchy. My first call to service in this delightful chapel found me ministering to a total congregation of four Italian waiters.

I was aboard the *Dagan* as chaplain and was witness to a most monstrous episode indicating how little progress has been made in human understanding and defeating anti-Semitism. I picked up the ship, a tramp steamer, in Montreal as she was on her way to Haifa, stopping at any point en route to pick up cargo to defray the cost of the trip. There were fourteen passengers with Captain Chaimov in charge and the voyage was delightful. I spent a great deal of time playing gin with him and living on the inevitable, sustaining life fluid of most sailors, good brandy and soda. A nasty storm arose which wrecked some equipment on the upper deck, tossed a bosun the length of the deck and during the tumultuous activity, a Spanish wiper went overboard and drowned. A wiper is one who works in the engine room. We were unable to recover his body and by sheer coincidence our next port of call was Barcelona, the home of the unfortunately deceased young man. On shore an inquest was held and witnesses called to officially determine the cause of death and the authorities agreed it was an accident caused by the storm at sea.

Just as the ship was about to sail, a delegation led by the chief of police of Barcelona and including members of the deceased's family, asked to come on board. They wanted to inspect the refrigerators of the Jewish ship so that they might be at ease that the Jews had not butchered the body in order to consume it on the trip. Anti-Semitism, 1961 vintage. Hatred for Jews is inspired by fear, fed by ignorance and the belief by too many Christians that only through their own church lies the road to righteousness.

I am very concerned about the young people who have turned away from their own religions to look for more inviting dogma. As life becomes too complicated, pressures too great to bear, they are ready to embrace any cult that offers easy answers and peace with a promise of security thrown in. They do not realize that in going out to look for something more inspiring and exotic, they are stepping over the treasure lying at their own front door. The new cults offer a doctrine which is a type of ultra-orthodoxy that shuts out reason. It is this loss of individual will that makes a movement like that of the Moonies so dangerous. Rev. S. M. Moon is raising up an army of dedicated, mindless zealots and the analogy to Nazism is frightening.

Orthodoxy carried to its ultimate extremes makes macabre bedfellows. There are Christian and Jewish sects that say the Holocaust was a punishment directed by God against the Jews. The Christian fanatics claim it is because the Jews have not kept the strictest injunctions of Jewish Law. Both offend me. Respectable scholars will agree that much of the dogma and theological approach of the Christian churches derives from Paul and his interpretation of the meanings of Jesus. I know this flies in the face of the Evangelical approach, but within the historical framework anyone aware of the Synoptic Gospels knows the first three, Matthew, Mark and Luke have one source. The Fourth Gospel, John, is based on the other three with interpolations which have been the basis for the most vicious anti-Semitism in the Christian Church.

If not for a series of circumstances involving Paul and the particular approach of the gospel writings, Jesus would have been remembered, but not in the way he is remembered now. The minute details of the New Testament Gospels are to be taken with a grain of salt. Jesus of Nazareth was created larger than life by a series of political incidents. If Jesus was not an Essene but a zealot bitterly opposed to Rome and head of a political movement against Rome, as some scholars now believe, He would have had a place in history with the Maccabees or Bar Kochba.

What happened was that the movement itself was destroyed first by the Jewish authorities themselves who collaborated with Rome and second, by Rome. I think it remains a matter of history that the fact of the collapse of the Jewish State in the battle against the Romans in the year seventy can be traced back to the middle sixties of the Common Era when Jews fought Jews because of the contention between the orthodox and conservative political viewpoints. There is a parallel which distresses me. Today, in Israel, the orthodox sit in solemn judgment on the rest of the Israelis to the detriment of the country and its future. Israel is not alone in this jeopardy. There is a totalitarian spirit reaching out across the earth from latter-day Communism, from Islam, from the Christian communities particularly in the United States where efforts are being made to base political movements on a strictly Christian approach to life. One of the great strengths of our country is the separation of Church and State, and it should remain so.

A considerable amount of damage has been done to religious understanding by simplistic movements in American society. For example, there is the Gospel approach, " . . . believe in the Lord, Jesus Christ and thou shall be saved." What should follow is that even if you do not believe you still have a chance for salvation which can come in other ways. I am protesting the restrictive covenant. Believing as I do in a loving God, I can hardly imagine He would exclude nine-tenths of the people of the earth from heaven simply because they do not subscribe to the dogma of one faith, one doctored faith in terms of its writings. People have found peace of mind and a way of life in many movements and if they do not attempt to force their beliefs on others, I think they too will find the road to salvation.

The pitfalls in these new religions arise when believers fail to examine the major inspirations in terms of the reverends, gurus or rabbis that started out preaching faith and ended up entrenched interests in the financial markets of the world. I fear the television religion salesmen who sell faith as if it were a new soul cleanser, thereby collecting millions of dollars. I would be willing to forget the fact that pastor this or reverend that or father something was creating a very lucrative business if I could be sure that all the funds flowed back through a legitimately religious approach to the world's problems. I approve the free enterprise

217

system even in the streets of the Lord, but too many of these religious movements find their way into political channels and use their accumulated membership to foster political policies that are anathema to a free society.

I think the concern of some of the Protestant and Jewish leadership is well taken when they protest Catholic intervention in federal legislation applying to abortion. I do not argue the moral issue of abortion but the weakening concept of the separation of church and state. One has only to look at the history of church-run countries to see the pitfalls. They differ from godless countries only in approach, not in the ultimate miseries of living. Disturbing also are the implications of the political support for Israel coming from the more fundamentalist Protestant groups of the country. With their belief that the Jewish State is a fulfillment of prophecy and that the conversion of all Jews to Christianity is a concomitant injunction of that belief, the prognosis for Jewish-Christian ecumenism is poor indeed. The fundamentalist approach does on occasion have its comic relief. Rev. Carl McIntire of South New Jersey, has supported Nixon totally until Nixon's trip to Communist China, has supported the Vietnam War and has borne the banner of Christianity against Communist Russia. His newest and very absurd conclusion is that Israel has been able to win several wars because of the intervention of UFO's piloted by angels, all maneuvered by God—encounters, I presume, of a fourth kind.

Areas of New Jersey seem to offer a hospitable climate to conservatism of all kinds, suffering the attentions of the John Birch Society, the Ku Klux Klan and an assortment of school boards that delight in banning books by whatever standards of censorship they dream up. I was very surprised during the tail end of the protest period to be asked to speak at a baccalaureate service in one community where my liberal attitudes were well established. When I arrived for the service I was told it was the students that invited me to speak, knowing of my interest in their opinions. The service was out of doors and replete with black robes and triumphal marches, but it also included guitar music played by long-haired musicians. I took my cue from the blend of old customs and new embellishments and based my talk that day on man's inhumanity to man, with illustrations out of my own experience, to emphasize my belief in the need for a less hypocritical approach on the part of society toward the Fatherhood of God and the Brotherhood of Man. The young people seemed quite pleased and congratulated me afterwards.

Because the fee was to be paid by the students I accepted a token fifty dollars. Several days later I received a letter with two checks, one from the senior class of the high school for twenty-five dollars and the other twenty-five from the local ministerium association. Apparently the ministers picked up half the tab because I was a minister, without knowing anything about me, because there was a curt note included from a clergyman. In an effort to be fair, he informed me that the students appeared to be pleased with what I had to say, but a number of ministers were disturbed by my views, and I paraphrase his observation, "It did not appear to be Bible Christianity." I was delighted to endorse the ministerial check to the pew fund of the African Methodist Episcopal Church in my community.

I will always be caught in the middle of the question of Messianic Promise, because with my unusual association with the Jewish community, whether the Messiah comes for the first time or the second time, I will be in trouble in either case.

CHAPTER 22

TALE ENDS

During Israel's early years, I arrived one morning on one of her ships and had to throw my weight around to be permitted to go ashore because it was the Jewish Sabbath. While the sailors, who during the early days of Israel's Merchant Marine included Spaniards and Greeks, were rowing me ashore, I stood up aft in the dinghy, wearing my Israeli naval uniform and feeling like Admiral Nelson reviewing the fleet at Trafalgar. A swell caught the dinghy and rammed the small vessel forward hitting the cement quay so that Lord Nelson found himself ignominiously deposited on his backside in the middle of the roaring water. I pulled myself up, waded onto the shore of Tel Aviv, wet, bedraggled with sand "squidging" in my shoes and walked to the Hotel Samuel where I was to stay for several days. After a thorough washing I made for the beach and a swim.

That evening, enjoying dinner with friends, someone asked me what I had done that day and I told them I had gone swimming.

"Did you swim in the pool at Herzliya or did you go up to Bat Yam?"

"Neither. I went swimming at the beach in Tel Aviv."

My hostess paled. "My God. It's polluted. One third of the

sewage of Tel Aviv empties untreated into the Mediterranean. It's against the law to swim there."

That confused me. "But there were thousands of people on the beach and in the water!"

"Those were the Oriental Jews and they don't understand about pollution."

"Well, if they aren't allowed to swim there, why are there lifeguards on the beach?"

"Because we don't want them to drown," was her explanation.

Up and down the shore of Israel there are "No Swimming" signs in three languages, and vigilant lifeguards on call while thousands of people camp on the beaches and go swimming. I suspect the intent in Israel is to put up the signs where they really do want you to swim.

I am constantly reminded that the Middle East is an area of surprises. Just when I begin to think I understand the Middle Eastern mind something happens to send me back to square one. A typical example is a story about an incident during the 1948 War. The Egyptians in the south had been cut off by the Israeli forces and were out of ammunition and supplies. The relief they were eagerly awaiting appeared when a number of trucks arrived. When unloaded it was discovered that King Farouk, illustrative of his military genius, had sent truckloads of chocolate and tea. One of the Egyptian officers receiving this windfall was Gamal Abdul Nasser. I would suspect the incident did nothing to dispel his disenchantment with his king and may even have helped to bring the revolution and the king's subsequent unemployment a little closer.

Understanding and empathy can be found in short supply even in the Holy Land, and one can meet innate cruelty under the strangest circumstances. In 1949 there were some rumors about the possible destruction of the holy places in Jerusalem as a result of the war. Israel was being charged with deliberate unconcern for Christian antiquities and shrines, and church dignitaries here at home were worried. As a matter of fact, there were those so anxious to believe the stories and discredit the Israelis, that a United Nations' commission, meeting outside of Israel and acting solely on rumor and lies, announced the Church Of The Nativity had been napalmed. So far as I know, that is still on the record.

Dr. Carl Herman Voss and I went to Israel to investigate and one of the people we went to see was George Hakim, Maronite Bishop of Haifa and Galilee. Years later, the Bishop was to become Patriarch Maximus of Lebanon and viciously anti-Israel, but in 1949 he was so pleased with the Israeli government that he joined Histraduth, the Labor Zionist group, which allowed him reduced rates in their various institutions around the country. He was satisfied with Israel's conduct during the war.

Our next visit was made to Monsignor Vergani, a Papal representative in Jerusalem. Dr. Voss and I kept a late afternoon appointment and found the meeting memorable. The Monsignor received us in his robes of office, wearing a large cross resting on his colored cassock, but the distinguished representative of Rome also had a pointed chin whisker and just a touch of a moustache, and my immediate reaction was, "My God! Cardinal Richelieu!" We began to discuss the Israeli atrocities but the Monsignor would discuss only one thing which bothered him enormously. In the Church of The Dormitian on Mt. Zion, marking the place where the Virgin Mother died, there is a statute of Mary in a reclining position, and the ivory hands of the Blessed Virgin were missing. It was the contention of Rome and Mons. Vergani that the Israelis had stolen the ivory hands. A very revealing assumption of guilt since the church itself had been overrun from several directions and by forces from both sides. The church was damaged and would be again by Arab shells in the 1967 War.

I was annoyed that the Monsignor was so concerned about a

statue when nearby was the Zion Gate through which many
Israeli soldiers had gone to rescue aged Jews from Old Jerusalem
and had died in the attempt. Eventually the Jordanian Legion was
to reduce that area to rubble. I gently mentioned to the Papal
representative that he seemed more concerned about the ivory
hands than the loss of those who died in the war. He raised his
hands benevolently as in the act of blessing us and said, "Aha, but
that is another question."

Perturbed about the problems of administering the Holy City
so that Jews as well as Christians would be allowed to visit the
Holy places, I placed the question directly to the Monsignor. Very
agitated he extended his hands outward, palms raised with fingers
curled up like claws and literally shouted toward the ceiling,
"Cannons, cannons, guns, guns." The evening was waning, casting that reddish glow characteristic of a Jerusalem sunset and
bathed the face of the Papal Vicar so that his likeness to Richelieu
took on a satanic tinge. I countered with, "We are speaking of
the city of Melchizedek, of Jerusalem, shalom, peace." He raised
his hands again, benignly saying, "Aha, but that is another question." We left. In the years that followed I have often visited the
shrine in the very beautiful Church Of The Dormitian, and the
Holy Mother does have her hands. Whether they are the originals
returned, or copies I cannot say.

The fact is that the Israelis fought hand to hand combat to
preserve the shrines with the result that they sustained a considerable loss of life. It certainly was not all altruism on the part of the
Jewish community that the holy places are so venerated. Actually,
Moslem and Christian structures are Jewish in their origins. The
Church Of The Holy Sepulcher stands on a Jewish necropolis
from before the time of Herod. If you are dealing with Golgotha,
with Calvary, the place of the execution of Jesus, you are dealing
not just with the death of One Jew, but of thousands who were
also executed there. Speak of the Kotel, the Wailing Wall or

Western Wall, Jews honor it as the wall of Herod's Temple. Christians respect it for the same reason because it was that Temple out of which Jesus drove the money changers. For Moslems the western wall and the south wall of Herod's Temple now sustain the platforms for the area that contains the Dome Of The Rock and el Aksa. Once upon a time, two Sultans were at war with each other. One of them, unable to get to Mecca, built his own shrine in Jerusalem called the Dome Of The Rock. From that rock Muhammad ascended to heaven on *Buraq*, which was a winged creature half mule, half donkey, with silken flanks and jeweled eyes. In the Persian tradition *Buraq* also had the face of a woman.

Jerusalem is the best example of the day to day relationships on both a social and business level, of the Christian Arabs, the Moslem Arabs, the Arab Jews and the Jews of western origin. The Moslem sabbath is Friday, the Jewish sabbath is Saturday and the Christian sabbath is Sunday and for business reasons it makes for a very amicable arrangement. On Saturday the Moslems are starting the first business day of the week. The Orthodox Jews all head for the Kotel to pray while the unobservant Jews come to Jerusalem to shop because their own communities are closed. The Christians shop on Saturday in preparation for their Sunday sabbath. It seems to the casual observer that all of Israel is in the Old City of Jerusalem on Saturday.

The bulk of the shops in the Old City are Arab-owned and bargaining goes on even though prices are fixed because it is an ancient tradition of the eastern marketplace. Everything is initially marked up one hundred percent and after haggling the dealer will settle for ten percent above fifty percent and everyone is aware of it but the game goes on and is a way of life in the commerce of the area. There are a good many places to eat and one can go to Kosta's near the Jaffa Gate where

TALE ENDS

Israelis, Greeks, Armenians and Moslems are all sitting at tables eating amid a babble of languages and a pantomime of waving hands.

Once in a while, there are bursts of temper as when orthodox Jews will charge through a crowd to get to the Wall to pray. I hope there is some tradition that one must rush to prayer or else it is just bad manners to say the least. I have also observed some altercations when Christians are in a procession of the Stations of the Cross, and once going up the Via Dolorosa I saw a Franciscan monk with his hands folded in prayer and obviously in a mild state of ecstacy, when an Arab delivering Coca Cola hit the monk on his back with a cart. There is very little respect for the beliefs of others even in the Holy City and the competition among the various religions is sometimes fierce and leading to disaffection among worshippers.

There are services held in the afternoon in the Sepulcher where the leader of the Armenian choir is urging his people to sing louder and drown out the Franciscans who are singing up on Calvary about one hundred and fifty feet away. The final touch comes when a black-robed man about 6'8" comes out ringing a large bell to advise both of them that it is the Greeks' turn. They have all been known to glorify God by hitting each other over the head with candles. The black Copts who spring from the Ethiopian Church have the back side of the Sepulcher and they are not too kindly treated by the six other groups who share that holy place. The stone of the tomb is shared by all and from the Copts' area you can touch the real stone. The Greeks have the forward part that is covered with marble and it is available to you when the curtain is parted. You are sprayed with a delightful rose water, and when you reach out to touch the Tomb of Christ it is rather difficult to feel because it is covered with the currency representing half the nations of the earth. The hint is obvious to all. You understand of course that everything is done in the name of a loving Jesus.

As a visitor you cannot tell how the Sepulcher is marked off into the seven realms governed by seven arms of Christianity. However, if a guardian of X faith goes into the territory of Y, an official from Y is apt to point out X's error forcefully with the end of a stave in the name of a Jesus whom only Ys understand. It is a fact of history that the Crimean War started because Eastern Orthodox people stole the gold star marking the place of the birth of Christ that had been placed there by those of the Roman rites. The Old City has always fascinated me. I have spent a great deal of time studying its archeology and have read almost everything written about it in English. I found out that two Crusader kings, followers of the Latin, or western rites, were buried at the Holy Sepulcher, and I could not find their tombs. I went to the Armenian authority on the subject and he pointed out that a wooden bench upon which I was seated was the grave of one of the kings. So much enmity existed between the Greek and Latin churches that all Latin markings had been removed from the sarcophagus which had been covered in marble, now covered over in wood and used as a bench.

The Russians are not represented at the Sepulcher itself, but on the side of a hill they have the Church of Magdaleine which is a beautiful church built in the Russian onion dome tradition, and there are daily services conducted, during which the bishops and archbishops are attired in the most extravagantly beautiful garments. I went to a service there one day and saw a petite nun holding alarge gold basin in which there was holy water. Unlike the western church where a silver hyssop is used to sprinkle holy water, the officiating patriarch was using what could be described as an oversized whisk broom which he would dip into the water and swish across the multitudes. The little nun was in the way, but it was fascinating to watch because she had learned to duck each time as the broom whisked past her nose. One must not lose one's sense of humor regarding religious observance even in the Holy Land. There is one story told about the religious approach to relics in this wondrous land. It is about a priest who was once sold the skull of a saint, an important find. Later he was sold the skull of the same saint when he was a child and the priest went home with a double header!

Every stick and stone in Jerusalem has its own history and becomes a demonstration of how a small area of the earth can become the world in microcosm. They say that if you sit at the Cafe de la Paix in Paris long enough, sooner or later you will meet everyone you know. In Jerusalem sit anywhere long enough and you can see the whole world go by. In the Sepulcher there is an urn that marks the center of the earth. The Moslems insist the center of the earth is marked by their mosque and since both centers are only a couple of hundred yards apart, I will not argue the accuracy of surveyors. One can sit at the Jaffa Gate and think back over three thousand years, remembering also that recently the Gate had to be made wider so Kaiser Wilhelm could ride through in a triumphal entry. Remembering also that General Allenby, recalling the Kaiser's action, chose to walk through.

People from all cultures find their way to Jerusalem. There is a sect of Japanese Christians from which five thousand people make a pilgrimage every year. I sometimes stand near the Hill of Evil Council, by Abu Tor, which faces the city from the south and look at this city that Sulemain built. It is hard to imagine that this tiny spot on the entire earth, a spot no bigger than Lefrak City, an apartment house complex in New York City, has been soaked in blood seventy-plus times and literally caused the death of millions of people. Millions more have been raised spiritually because of that tiny patch of land. The stones of Jerusalem are piled one upon the other through the reaches of history and except for peripheral situations on the far side of the earth, every bit of history in the end tends in its direction.

I have friends who live in Jerusalem and are startled when I remind them it is sacred soil upon which they move and take for granted. There are those too who think constantly in religious terms. I am reminded of a Greek nun who sits every single hour of the day on a bench in the corner of the Church of the Holy Sepulcher and says her prayers, hardly seeming to take the time for the needs of living. I have watched other people approach the sacred spots, whatever their religious origin, in a state of awe. I have seen American Jews, who had never acknowledged themselves to be remotely religious, do very uncharacteristic things once they are exposed to the mystique that is Jerusalem. Some who do not even know the simple blessing over bread, would leap to the nearest store to purchase a yarmulke or prayer shawl before going to the Western Wall. Neither would they ever be able to fathom the overwhelming response of religious identification they feel in spite of their sophistication. The tragedy of Jerusalem lies in that, though the Old City and the New City are physically one, it is divided by the individual dogmas of those who are fanatically convinced that only they have the truth given only to them by God.

The city's inhabitants also have their pragmatic interests. There is a cynicism that shocks me as when I climb one particular street to see there is an "Eighth Station Of The Cross Souvenir Shop." I can almost see the Arab merchant running out to Jesus to offer a coke as He went by carrying the cross, or pushing Gaza brass on the local prophet. There are also the "true pieces of the cross" offered for sale, which if laid end to end could rebuild the Atlantic City boardwalk. There is also the case of the mayor of Bethlehem who comes to the United States and gets prominent Catholics like Gov. Byrne of New Jersey to support a program to raise fifty million dollars to build an underground garage in Manager Square. I could rebuild the entire church for that amount, but there is a tendency to think up gimmicks and good people are very vulnerable.

Recently, before a trip to Israel, I asked a lady what I could bring back for her and being mortally ill, she asked me to bring her water from the Jordan River to cure her disease. It was used at her funeral service. There are many more such commercial ventures that thrive on the religious pilgrims. Just as in Rome during Holy Week, in Jerusalem one can buy a little wax lamb blessed by the Pope and thereby endowed with all sorts of miraculous powers. The rabbinate in Israel has built up quite an industry selling little bags of earth so that orthodox Jews around the world can be buried with a piece of the Holy Land. Jerusalem will survive everything.

In the Jewish as well as the Christian tradition, it is believed that after the Messiah comes, judgment will be held in the Valley of Jehoshafat which is between the city and the Mt. Of Olives. One day I was lecturing in front of the Intercontinental Hotel built in King Hussein's time, and explaining that in the Jewish tradition you must burrow through the earth from your burial place to reach Jehoshafat for the Day of Judgment. I flippantly observed that I would hope to be buried on Mt. Herzl so I would not have to dig so far. One Yeshiva student asked me how God would be able to accommodate all the millions of souls in one small spot. My response was, "If He can bring them all together, he can find the room," like the Holy City, where there is room for everyone.

CHAPTER 23

TODAY GUNS, TOMORROW BUTTER

Living in Israel means living under constant security. While walking home late at night I come upon elderly men with guns slung over their shoulders while patrolling empty streets, there is a momentary shock, but three or four days later the home guard fades into the background. Women become accustomed to opening their purses and shopping bags before entering a market or theater. Men are searched as well and those wearing tight blue jeans must open the little bags they often carry to hold their cigarettes and such. Identification papers must be produced on demand in public places and often at private functions, if deemed necessary because of the prominence of someone in attendance. Private home parties usually have need for security because of the ease with which an outsider may slip in and leave something on a table or shove something lethal into a loosely closed package. You could call for a security guard but usually there is some member of the family able to serve in that capacity.

In the north, on the kibbutzim, every father in every family wears a pistol and the mother often keeps one in her purse. If they leave the kibbutz to shop, the gun is kept handy on the seat next to the driver and slipped casually into a pocket before entering a store. One gets used to firearms. Public buses inevitably have half a dozen or so Israeli soldiers on board with their guns and ammunition which they must keep with them at all times, even when on leave at home. People coming from a western culture and unused to such a constant display of self-defense become used to it quickly.

Every community has its bomb shelters and in some areas of the north, if tension is apparent because of some recent or expected terrorism, the children sleep underground. If there is shelling in a border area, sleeping in or rushing for the shelters during the day becomes a way of life. Bomb shelters are not allowed to decay or become exhibits or relics of another era for the curious tourists, as they so fortunately have in other places in the world. Israeli shelters are kept maintained and stocked for instant use. Tourist buses pass cement outcroppings on the landscape that are decorated with all sorts of colorful, happy pictures painted upon them and are shaken up when told these seemingly innocuous structures have a grim lifesaving function.

There are many Arab quarters tourists may visit with impunity. They are of course for business or shopping and even if the Arabs harbored any animosities they would hardly make them apparent. In any case, Arabs are a courteous people by nature if not unduly antagonized. My own association with the Arab community had been generally serene for some years, and they just assumed I was an American clergyman who chose to live part of the year in Israel. Between 1948 and the '67 War I never discussed politics except in a very desultory fashion, with the Arab leaders who were my friends. The general Arab population in Israel during that period of time knew very little of what was happening beyond a few hundred feet from their shops. After the war in 1967 the country as a whole became more polarized with an increasing political awareness on the part of Arab citizens.

Arab suspicion grew about my presumed political nonalliance and culminated, coincidentally, at the time of what the Israeli and world press referred to as the Capucci Affair in 1974. That was the case of the presumably Catholic bishop who was caught using his religious freedom of movement to smuggle ammunition and military weapons into the Old City for use by Arab terrorists. He received a twelve year prison sentence and was freed by the Israelis at the request of the Pope in 1977, with the proviso that he be confined to Rome and more peaceful pursuits. Some sloppy reporting failed to record that Capucci was really Capudji and a bishop from the Syrian Melchite part of the Catholic Church in Rome.

My pro-Israel sentiments became apparent to the church and Arab communities when I did not conceal my delight with the Israeli war victories. The fact that my relationship with Israel was more than that of a sideline rooter came when the day Bishop Capudji was arrested and I was awarded the Medal of Jerusalem by Teddy Kollek for my services to the founding of the country.

I was advised by friends to move with caution in the Arab community thereafter, but I was not concerned until I had an unpleasant experience that jolted me into being less sanguine about my safety. I had taken a group of the Mission youngsters to a restaurant in Acre which was serviced by Arabs. Unless there is some sort of pastry I do not eat desserts in Israel. There is no quality control over canned fruit and I despise the stuff. I think the worst thing Israel could do to her enemies short of declaring war would be to send them boatloads of canned grapefruit. That day in Acre, the dessert was canned grapefruit sections, and there was one fellow at the table with an enormous capacity for food and whatever I could not or would not eat I would pass to him. He uttered a cry of anguish at the first spoonful and an immediate investigation revealed splinters of glass underneath the fruit. Luckily the young man did not get hurt. The police found it was the only bowl of the sixty to have been served that day that contained the glass slivers. Further investigation did not turn up the criminal, but it did serve to endow me with a renewed sense of caution the like of which I had not found necessary since the British left the country.

To live in Israel is for me, at least, to live with the Holocaust, since there is always some incident to bring its aftermath home to me. When the first West German Ambassador came to Israel, around 1965 I think, it was preceded by intense debate and emotional opposition throughout the country on the part of the Jewish population. The horrors were all too new with the remnants of the attempted genocide still living all around us with its scars. At the Ambassador's first public appearance he was heralded by a band playing *Deutschland Uber Alles* and while some people stiffened up perceptibly and others looked grim, there were many more who were dissolved in tears and shaken with a passion that could not be encompassed with mere words. Leaflets bearing pictures of the armbands worn by Jews in the ghettos were thrown from the roof-tops of the buildings bordering on Zion Square. My own reaction was hard to control as I watched the play of emotions on the faces of those around me, yet I know prejudices must cease with future generations.

Last summer a woman came to me in Israel. I was tired, had paper work to catch up on and had left word that I was not to be disturbed, but she became hysterical when told I would not see her, so of course I did. While on board the *Exodus* a woman died giving birth to a son who later died in a British hospital. What I had not known was that she left a husband and a two and a half year old daughter and it was that child now in her thirties who wanted to see me. She had been born in a freight car while her parents were running away from Siberia and the Russians, to find allies in the south. She was here to see me because her father has absolutely refused to speak to her of her mother and the *Exodus* period of his life and she felt the need to fill the gaps. I told her all I remembered.

There is a need to know the truth about the Holocaust on many levels. I believe those who have lived through it have an obligation to make their experiences known from its origins, so their children will understand and cherish their present freedoms and become part of the cadre that will fight any symptoms of future political or religious extremism. The history of the Holocaust must be taught to all of our children in the schools until they understand clearly that it can happen not only to "them" but to "us" as well. It must be taught so that the link between the ballot box and those who would play havoc with our civil rights is recognized, and the right to vote is seen as a treasured obligation, a weapon against tyranny, instead of an indulgence if it is not raining on election day.

I was lecturing on the Holocaust at a university in Houston, Texas and was surprised and pleased to find that most of the students present were not Jewish. I always ask about backgrounds to be able to engage their interest on a more personal level. One lad in the back of the room looked like a Nazi's dream of the perfect Aryan-blonde, sturdy and athletic. After the lecture he came up to me and apologized for not asking any questions because he did not know what questions to ask. I asked him what prompted him to sign up for the course. He explained he had been sitting in the Commons with friends, trying to fill out his class schedule with some electives and saw the subject: Literature of the Holocaust. He asked his friends what it was and they guessed it must be books such as *Towering Inferno, Airport* or *Earthquake,* so he decided to take the program. By the end of the week he began to find the subject interesting and was enjoying the class.

Here at home I am still concerned about the attempt at proselytizing coming from any Christian, but even more incensed when it is directed at Jews. They have been sufficiently assaulted by the gentile community and to compound that crime by an effort to subvert their youth, I find outrageous in the extreme. I have been

234

encouraged by indications that young Jews who have been flound-ering in their faith have been returning to the fold. I would credit this awakening to efforts such as those expended by the Luba-vitcher Community and its Mitzvahmobile. I was delighted by a personal encounter with these dedicated people.

I own a very long, wonderfully warm overcoat, one among many sold cheaply, that had been dug out of British surplus to be used by Israeli soldiers on the Golan Heights. They were originally made to be worn by the British Home Guard in World War II. Just as was found at Ft. Myer, Virginia, many years after the Civil War, that there were more saddles in stock than were used during the entire war, so the British overdid the stocking of long over-coats. My particular model was adorned by me with several Israeli shoulder patches. One very bitter cold day, I was walking down Fifth Avenue in New York with a group of my Jewish students, on the way to an Israeli restaurant for lunch. As we were moving down the street a Mitzvahmobile drove up, stopped and some Yeshiva Bucherim dropped off. Let me stop here for a glossary of terms. The Lubavitcher are a sect of orthodox Jews; a mitzvah is a good deed, hence a Mitzvah-Mobile is a good deed on wheels; a yeshiva is a school for Talmudic study; bucherim is plural for bucher which means student who, in my observation this day on Fifth Avenue, all wear the same clothes in the same size, and all their hats are two inches too small for their heads. What they lack in sartorial elegance they make up for in joyous dedication to their faith and a willingness to share it with other Jews. Their proce-dure is open, simple and in no way becomes the obnoxious afflic-tion of unwanted attentions practiced by many sects.

One of the bucherim came over to Gary, one of my students, and asked him if he were Jewish, which he was. He then turned to Saliba who though Christian, spoke Hebrew in reply thereby confusing the situation considerably. The purpose of the question is that if you are Jewish and interested, you are invited into the

GRAUEL

Mitzvahmobile and given literature, candles and simple candlesticks for sabbath use. You are encouraged to re-examine your Jewish heritage and learn more about yourself and your Jewish origins. One young man turned to me in great anticipation seeing my Israeli shoulder patches, my long white hair and my white beard. What he could not see was my turned clerical collar because my coat was closed against the cold. He asked if I were a Jew, whereupon I opened my coat exposing my collar and the large cross on my chest saying in Yiddish as I did so, "Siz shwere tzu zein ein goyisher goluch." (It's hard to be a gentile priest.) He wheeled in his tracks and made for the sanity of the Mitzvahmobile, nearly going through a bank's glass window in the process.

When I am asked why I never chose to live in Israel permanently, if I am being perfectly honest, the answer is I could not stand living there. I thought as an American I had seen red tape at its worst, but the Israelis have refined it to an art. Some day they will either strangle in it or do away with most of it. I am resigned to the fact that in a democratic country some red tape is an inalienable right. I also find I am too old to have the patience for queuing up for everything because I am too tired for all the accompanying pushing and shoving. The bureaucracy has spread from one end of the country to the other infecting not only Jews, but Arabs and Christians as well.

I can see the rest of my life, for whatever years are left to me by the Grace of God, spent in the United States continuing to speak out for Israel and her place in the universe, and indulging Jewish consciousness raising groups with such weighty discussions as, Psychiatry and Portnoy's mother. I will spend my winters looking forward to my summers in Israel and my summers looking forward to going home to New Jersey. At this moment, President Sadat of Egypt and Prime Minister Menachem Begin of Israel have come together, through a miracle, to talk of peace. I can still hear Moshe Sharett's answer to me when I asked him about peace. "Not in our lifetime, Jochanan." Please God he was wrong. Shalom.

Pine Brook, Tinton Falls, N.J.
November 19, 1977

INDEX

238

INDEX

GRAUEL